ABSOLUTELY EVERYTHING!

FOR 11–14s

THROUGH THE BIBLE IN 11 GAME-BASED SESSIONS

TERRY CLUTTERHAM

First published in 2000 by CPAS
Reprinted 2000, 2001, 2004 by Scripture Union
This edition copyright © 2011 Scripture Union

ISBN 978 1 84427 642 4

Scripture Union
207–209 Queensway, Bletchley, Milton Keynes, MK2 2EB
Email: info@scriptureunion.org.uk
Website: www.scriptureunion.org.uk

Scripture Union Australia
Locked Bag 2, Central Coast Business Centre, NSW 2252
Website: www.scriptureunion.org.au

Scripture Union USA
PO Box 987, Valley Forge, PA 19482
Website: www.scriptureunion.org

Bible text is from The Contemporary English Version © 1997 British and
Foreign Bible Society

Historical dates are from *Pocket Dates and Events*, David Herman, © 1994
Kingfisher Books

British Library Cataloguing-in-Publication Data
A catalogue record for this book is available from the British Library.

Written by Terry Clutterham
Additional material by Andrew Haslam
Design by Phil Grundy
Illustrations by Simon Smith
Printed by Tien Wah Press

With thanks to David Bell, Jo Campbell, Jenny Charteris, Sue Clutterham,
Dick Farr, Geoff Harley-Mason, Philip Mounstephen, Andrew Petit and
Hannah Redman for their constructive critiques of the material.

Scripture Union is an international charity working with churches in
more than 130 countries, providing resources to bring the good news of
Jesus Christ to children, young people and families and to encourage
them to develop spiritually through the Bible and prayer.

As well as our network of volunteers, staff and associates who run
holidays, church-based events and school Christian groups, we produce a
wide range of publications and support those who use our resources
through training programmes.

CONTENTS

GOD CREATES - GOD PROMISES - GOD JUDGES

GOD SAVES - GOD SHOWS WHO HE IS

DOING ABSOLUTELY EVERYTHING!

The Bible is a big, complicated book. No wonder most young people (and adults too) struggle with it, give up on it, or ignore it altogether – thousands of pages and tiny black print about life a million years ago.

Absolutely Everything! is designed to help you and your young people to:

• see the Bible as one big story
• wonder at the God who creates, makes promises, shows who he is, judges and saves
• understand better the significance of what Jesus did, is doing and will do
• want to be and remain on God's side in this big story
• trace the five themes of 'creation', 'promise', 'revelation', 'judgement' and 'salvation' in your own lives, and so be more aware of God's work in and around you, and more open to it.

SESSION OUTLINE

Each learning session has a game or activity (called **Scheme**) as its main feature. Many of the key events in the Bible involve dramatic action, spoken words and taking sides, as games do. That is great as 11–14s learn best by being actively involved in fun situations. Games can provide the mix of skills, attitudes and knowledge that is vital for memorable learning to take place.

However, there are other elements in each session, all nicely beginning with 's' so that you can remember them.

Time allocations
A clock symbol will indicate suggested time allocation for each Scene-setter, Scheme, Shout, Symbol, Scoreboard and Space activity.

Scene-setter
An introduction to the part of the Bible you're going to explore

Scheme
The game-based activity that unpacks the Bible events

Shout
A snappy memory-jogger that summarises the session's learning

Symbol
A visual memory-jogger for this part of the big story (possibly scanned into your computer, coloured and manipulated to add interest, or drawn or painted freehand, or colour photocopied)

Scoreboard
A visual way of collecting themes every time the group comes across them (see page 7)

Space
Time for group members to reflect on the five themes and on their own lives with God

Note that the point of the Bible episodes isn't to illustrate the five themes – God will be saying and doing other things too! No, the point is to recognise that God is the 'hero' of everything that happens in the Bible, to discover a little of what he is like, and to demonstrate that he doesn't change.

DIFFERENT FACES, DIFFERENT SPACES

Absolutely Everything! works well for midweek or Sunday group sessions, weekends away with a group and week-long residentials. There is enough material here for at least 11 one-hour learning sessions. If you don't have an hour, do a shortened version, for example using just the **Scene-setter**, the **Scheme** and the **Space** at the end.

Midweek or Sunday groups

Don't try to use all 11 sessions one after the other. You could split them into clumps of three or four, covering all 11 over a period of, say, six months.

Weekend away

Don't try to fit all 11 sessions into one weekend! Every part of the Bible is vitally important but you'll just have to be selective. For instance, if you have four learning sessions, try:

1 **Amazing days** (a light, fun activity that will 'break the ice' and introduce the themes)
2 **Civilization?** (what went wrong with people and the world)
8 **Kingdom rules** (Jesus' life, death and resurrection)
10 **Weird, wild and wonderful** (when the creating, promising, revealing, judging and saving will all come to a climax).

Organise a 'Big questions' graffiti wall on which group members can write up anything that's puzzling them about God and life. Alternatively, try a 'Big questions' box which will allow group members to remain anonymous. Exploring the big themes in the big, true story can prompt big questions. Group together questions on a similar theme before attempting to answer them.

Week-long residential activity

Do the lot! Because the sessions are activity-based, you can do two of them each day with no risk of boredom. Try a programme like the one opposite.

Use different groupings of people creatively throughout the week. For instance:

- Start the *Absolutely Everything!* sessions all together. Then, for the **Space** activity, divide into small groups to encourage everyone to think and talk about the themes in relation to their own life.

- Invite individuals to go off alone to read, think and pray about the key Bible verses mentioned in the main session. They could make notes in an *Absolutely Everything!* notepad, if you have a fairly 'booky' crowd who would find this kind of 'spiritual journal' helpful.

- Towards the end of the week, let them form friendship groups to talk about what they have discovered from the Bible and the difference it might make to their lives. They might share something from their notepads.

PREPARATION

Each learning session will involve around two hours' preparation, divided up in this way:

- 30 minutes to explore the Bible for yourself, to complete the Leader Theme Card (see page 7) and to pray

- 30 minutes to choose your activities and to familiarise yourself with the session outline

- one hour to prepare any materials you may need to run the session.

WEEK-LONG RESIDENTIAL ACTIVITY PROGRAMME

EVENING DAY 1
1 'AMAZING DAYS!'

DAY 2
2 'CIVILIZATION'
3 'GOING PLACES'

DAY 3
4 'FREE AT LAST!'
5 'TRIBAL RIVALS'

DAY 4
6 'EXILE'
7 'GATES AND WALLS'

DAY 5
MORNING OFF/
DAY TRIP OUT
8 'KINGDOM RULES'

DAY 6
9 'EARLY CHURCHES'
10 'WEIRD, WILD AND WONDERFUL'

DAY 7
11 'THE WHOLE STORY'
MASSIVE ABSOLUTELY
EVERYTHING! CELEBRATION

The right-hand column shows you one way to create a stunning theme scoreboard. Use it as a model to create your own stylish scoreboard design. This is used in each session to help the group members trace the five *Absolutely Everything!* themes through the Bible.

LEADER THEME CARD

SESSION NAME

SESSION DATE

GOD CREATES

GOD PROMISES

GOD SHOWS WHO HE IS

GOD JUDGES

GOD SAVES

SCOREBOARD

SESSION NAME

SESSION DATE

GOD CREATES

GOD PROMISES

GOD SHOWS WHO HE IS

GOD JUDGES

GOD SAVES

1 AMAZING DAYS!

READ
GENESIS 1:1 – 2:3
PSALM 8
EPHESIANS 1:3–10

CREATION

AIMS

To help group members:

- understand that the Bible is about one God who, amongst other things, is always creating, promising, showing who he is, judging and saving
- see that the Bible is also about many individuals and peoples who either lived God's way or didn't
- fix the amazing creation days in their minds
- wonder at the incredible variety of all that God made from nothing

SCOPE

Before the creation of the world, God planned for there to be people he could call his own. With lavish generosity, he made an amazing place for them to belong, where they could both see and meet him.

BIBLE BASE

Genesis 1:1 – 2:3; Psalm 8; Ephesians 1:3–10

MATERIALS AND EQUIPMENT

Each game team will need:

- ▢ a dice
- ▢ an 'Amazing days!' game card (page 11)
- ▢ a Bible
- ▢ a carrier bag
- ▢ a pen

For your own preparation and for other parts of the session, you'll need:

- ▢ a copy of the Leader Theme Card (page 7) and a Bible
- ▢ a spaceperson costume (well, improvise!)
- ▢ an overhead projector and screen (optional)
- ▢ thick felt-tip pens
- ▢ the Theme Scoreboard (see page 7)
  the metrical version of Psalm 8 (from **Space** on page 10) written up on a large sheet of paper or on an overhead projector acetate
- ▢ an enlarged version of the session **Symbol** and **Shout** (page 12) on overhead projector acetate or paper

PREPARATION

DO 'YOUR OWN TIME WITH GOD' (SEE BELOW). FAMILIARISE YOURSELF WITH THE SESSION OUTLINE. GET TOGETHER ALL THE MATERIALS AND EQUIPMENT YOU NEED.

YOUR OWN TIME WITH GOD

Reflect on anything you have enjoyed of God's creation today – the air you have breathed, the sky you may have taken for granted, the beauty of any water you have walked or driven past, the colours of the trees and the variety of the plants, the sun that has sustained life (even if you haven't seen much of it!), the animals and birds you have noticed, and friends whose company you have appreciated. Think of the young people in your group as unique, valuable and loved parts of creation. Thank God for creating all this, and for wanting you and your group members to be his people in it.

Read Ephesians 1:3–10 and Genesis 1:1 – 2:3, pausing to note down on your Leader Theme Card any echoes of the five themes you discover. Psalm 8 calls us to respond to all this. As you read it, pause at the end of each sentence or verse. Praise God for what those words tell us about him and for how you have seen that they are true.

Pray that your young people will be awe-struck by our Creator God who never changes, who has involved Bible characters in bringing about 'all that he has planned' (Ephesians 1:10), and wants to involve us in it, too.

READ
EPHESIANS 1:3—10
GENESIS 2:1—3

Throughout this session one leader should remain dressed as a spaceperson. (Well, why not?)

SCENE-SETTER

Tell your group that you're going to explore the Bible from start to finish – it's the huge, true story of absolutely everything! The Bible tells us absolutely everything we need to know about God and his amazing vast plan, and about how we can be part of it, on God's side.

Challenge everyone to shout out the names of 20 different Bible characters within two minutes. Ask: 'Suppose the Bible isn't just a random set of people's life-stories, but all one big story. What do you think the one story is about?' Listen to their suggestions and encourage them to think further.

Explain that the Bible is made up of the true life-stories of lots of different characters, but it's also one big story of how God creates, saves and shapes people to be his own, start to finish.

SYMBOL AND SHOUT

Display the 'Amazing days!' **Symbol** (page 12), either on an overhead projector acetate or on a large sheet of paper, and get everyone to chant the **Shout** until they know it by heart. Leave the **Symbol** and **Shout** displayed for the rest of the session.

SCHEME

Play this game in one or more teams of up to four people. Ideally you will have one adult leader per team to help. (This could be a good opportunity to call on others in the church who might be willing to 'help out' but not to 'lead'.) If you have more than one team, decide whether you want to make the activity competitive or not. If not, race all the teams against the clock.

Group members should first decide who will do each of the following key jobs for their teams: team leader, Bible reader, listener and writer. If there are fewer than four in the team, double up tasks. The team leader reads out what the card says and keeps the action moving.

Give each team a game card, dice, pen, carrier bag and Bible. Explain that they are going to work their way through the days of creation. When they have completed all the activities for a day, they must get close to you or another leader so you can watch them roll the dice. They must throw the number of the next day before going on to it.

Say that the game they're about to play will take them back to where the big story all began. Before anything else happened, God chose people to be on his side in the big story. But they would need a brilliant place to belong…

Get the spaceperson to walk forward deliberately and read Ephesians 1:3–10 very dramatically. (If you have the time and equipment, use background music and visuals to add to the effect.) The moment the Bible reading finishes the teams can begin rolling their dice for Day 1.

As each team finishes, get the team members to rest, because that's what God did on the seventh day. When everyone has finished, read out Genesis 2:1–3.

10

SCOREBOARD

Display the Theme Scoreboard, probably on the floor to start with, but later on the wall. Say that it will be displayed throughout your *Absolutely Everything!* sessions so that you can add discoveries about God at any time. Explain the five themes in your own words, using these descriptions to help you:

- **God creates** He makes what is good from nothing, or from something bad, or from something not so good.

- **God promises** He says what will definitely happen, or does things which show the even better things he'll do later.

- **God shows who he is** God lets people know who he is and what he's like.

- **God judges** God is for what's right and against what's wrong; wrong will always be punished in the end.

- **God saves** God makes his people safe from the very worst that can happen to them.

Say that God does these five things – and much more besides – all the way through the Bible because that's what he's like. But you and your group will try to discover in what ways he does them, at different points of the Bible story.

Together, look at each theme in turn, thinking how God is doing that thing in this part of the Bible, if he is. Write words or short phrases in the right theme space on the Scoreboard, to describe exactly what he does.

 10

SPACE

Use this metrical, rap version of Psalm 8. If you have up to four group members, get them to practise it together, with one leading and everyone else shouting the words in bold print. Could they make up a dance or some actions for it that have street cred? If you have more than four group members, divide into the same small groups as for the **Scheme**.

Just look at the sky
No one's greater than you, Lord
The moon floating by
No one's safer than you, Lord
The stars right up high
No one's stronger than you,
Just you,
Only you
Didn't use
Super-glue.

And even before birth
No one's greater than you, Lord
You give us all worth
No one's safer than you, Lord
We rule the whole earth
But no one's stronger than you,
Just you,
Only you
Didn't use
Super-glue.

Don't be afraid to let them have a bit of fun! This is a deliberately light way of rounding off this first session, though in future sessions you will invite more of a response.

Finish by doing the 'Amazing days!' **Shout** together (page 12).

GAME CARD

YOU MUST=
- work together as a team
- throw the right number for the 'amazing day' before you start the day's activities, so get a one for Day 1, then a two for Day 2, and so on
- work through the days in order

- tick each activity as you complete it
- get within sight of a leader after you have completed each day's activities, so that you can roll for the next day.

....

DAY 1
- ☐ Take it in turns to roll the dice until you throw a one.
- ☐ Get someone to read Genesis 1:1–5.
- ☐ Listen for what God created on this day and write it here.

....

- ☐ Light travels more than 300,000 km (nearly eight times round the world) in one second.
  Find something to put in your bag that is transparent – it lets light travel through it.

DAY 2
- ☐ Take it in turns to roll the dice until you throw a two.
- ☐ Get someone to read Genesis 1:6–8.
- ☐ Listen for what God created on this day and write it here.

....

- ☐ Oxygen makes up 21 per cent of the air. It is vital for human and animal life. Put something in your bag that creates so much air resistance that it takes three seconds or more to fall to the ground when dropped from the height of the top of the door.

DAY 3
- ☐ Take it in turns to roll the dice until you throw a three.
- ☐ Get someone to read Genesis 1:9–13.
- ☐ Listen for what God created on this day and write it here.

....

- ☐ Over 400,000 different kinds of plant are known to us. Put something in your bag that is made from a plant.

DAY 4
- ☐ Take it in turns to roll the dice until you throw a four.
- ☐ Get someone to read Genesis 1:14–19.
- ☐ Listen for what God created on this day and write it here.

....

- ☐ The temperature at the very centre of the sun is around 15,000,000°C. Put something in your bag that was made by being heated up.

DAY 5
- ☐ Take it in turns to roll the dice until you throw a five.
- ☐ Get someone to read Genesis 1:20–23.
- ☐ Listen for what God created on this day and write it here.

....

- ☐ There are about 9,000 different species of bird in the world. Write in the box below seven kinds of bird in order of size – smallest to biggest.

1 ....

2 ....

3 ....

4 ....

5 ....

6 ....

7 ....

DAY 6
- ☐ Take it in turns to roll the dice until you throw a six.
- ☐ Get someone to read Genesis 1:24–31.
- ☐ Listen for what God created on this day and write it here.

....

- ☐ Put something in the bag to show that each team member is different from all the rest.
- ☐ Now get your bag, this card, your pen and Bible back to your leader as quickly as possible! And rest.

AMAZING DAYS!

SIX AMAZING DAYS FOR CREATION, FOLLOWED BY ONE FOR RELAXATION –

BEFORE HIS REST GOD WORKED HIS BEST.

THE RESULTS OF REBELLING AGAINST GOD

AIMS

To help group members:
- be clear that God judges people for what they do, whether good or bad
- recognise that sin is real and affects the lives of us all

SCOPE

The Tower of Babel was people's attempt to 'reach for the stars' without God. In the end they paid dearly.

BIBLE BASE

Genesis 11:1–9; Romans 3:9–26

MATERIALS AND EQUIPMENT

For your own preparation and for other parts of the session, you'll need:

- your Leader Theme Card (page 7) and Bible
- overhead projector and screen (optional)
- judge's gear (optional)
- several reels of sticky tape
- several reels of parcel tape
- a few balls of string
- piles of newspapers
- heaps of old magazines
- lots of light paper or plastic junk (no lead drainpipes!)
- several pairs of scissors
- small sticky labels
- pens
- tape measure or ruler
- kitchen timer, alarm clock or other noisy way of timing events
- a few large sheets of blank paper
- Grunt'n'stuff Cards photocopied and cut up (page 16), one card per group member
- edible treasure (eg chocolate golden coins)
- Genesis 3:15 on overhead projector acetate or large sheet of paper
- enlarged version of the session **Symbol** and **Shout** (page 17) on overhead projector acetate or paper
- the Theme Scoreboard
- thick felt-tip pens

PREPARATION

DO 'YOUR OWN TIME WITH GOD' (SEE BELOW). FAMILIARISE YOURSELF WITH THE SESSION OUTLINE. MAKE SURE YOU GRASP THE SHAPE OF THE SESSION SO THAT YOU KEEP IT ON TRACK. GET TOGETHER ALL THE MATERIALS AND EQUIPMENT YOU NEED.

YOUR OWN TIME WITH GOD

Read Genesis 11:1–9. People chose their own way rather than God's for the sake of 'progress' (verses 3,4). God judged them and found them guilty (verses 5,7,8). Unity became disunity; clarity smudged over into confusion; community disintegrated into isolation; desire for stability gave way to insecurity; self-glorification meant eventual humiliation. However, God had a way of putting things right again. Enjoy Romans 3:9–26.

Fill in your Leader Theme Card for these Bible passages and simply thank God for Jesus. Pray that, through this session, your group members will grasp something of the reality of sin and their own need of forgiveness.

READ
GENESIS 11:1–9
ROMANS 3:9–26

CIVILISATION?

Throughout this session one leader should be dressed as a judge.
(Bizarre? You haven't seen anything yet!)

SCENE-SETTER

Divide your group into teams. It doesn't matter if there are only two teams of two. Give each team a pair of scissors, some sticky tape and a newspaper. Challenge them to build the tallest free-standing tower out of newspaper in five minutes. When the time is up, measure the towers and congratulate the winners.

SYMBOL AND SHOUT

Display the 'Civilization?' **Symbol** and **Shout** (page 17). Have fun learning the **Shout** together. Leave the **Symbol** and **Shout** on display for the rest of the session.

Introduce the **Scheme** in this way: *People were the best of God's creation. God wanted them to stay close to him, but they chose to go their own way. So God judged them. They were in the wrong and would suffer. But even then, God promised... (Show Genesis 3:15 on an acetate or large sheet of paper.) In the future there would be someone who would 'crush the head' of wrong once and for all. Meanwhile people got worse and worse until God washed the whole lot away in a flood and started again. Well, not quite the whole lot. God saved one man – Noah – and his family. But the happy story didn't last long. After Noah, people decided to build a tower and be 'civilized'...*

SCHEME

Get your small teams to join together into one big team for a huge challenge. Explain the whole task first. They must stick all their mini-towers together to make one big tower, then carry on building it right to the ceiling. (Set another target if this is not possible in your meeting place.) Point out any safety limits, for example avoiding any light fittings. (You will need to keep an eye on safety throughout the activity). Suggest that they stick structures to the bottom of their tower and gradually raise it up rather than piling up chairs and tables to try to reach the ceiling!

Explain that they will have to write a message to the world and stick it on the very top of their tower: 'Look! Aren't we brilliant!' If they think carefully about it, they will realise that they have to stick the message on the construction before it gets too high, but let them work this out for themselves or become horribly frustrated.

Carry out this **Scheme** challenge by working through the following rounds.

ROUND 1

Get your judge to stand high up and read out Genesis 11:1–4. He or she should then set the timer to go off five minutes before the end of your **Scheme** time. Explain to the group members that when the alarm sounds, their time will be up. Get them started on building but stop them after about five minutes.

ROUND 2

The judge should stand high up again and read out Genesis 11:5. Then he or she comes down and measures the tower, generally making fun of it for not being that high – even if it *is* high!

ROUND 3

Now the judge stands high up and reads out Genesis 11:6,7. Get everyone to pick a Grunt'n'stuff Card at random. By only making the noise printed on their cards, they have to gather themselves into small teams of like-sounding people – all of which is a massive distraction from the building task and will make some group members complain like crazy! (In case you're wondering, Burblers vibrate their lips with their fingers and hum!)

Give each team a pen and a set of sticky labels. Each person must wear a sticky label to show which language group they belong to. As soon as they are wearing a label, they can join in with building the big tower again. However, they can now only communicate with each other or other teams by using their sound. Anyone caught using normal language is disqualified. As soon as the timer alarm goes off, stop everyone working and check the height of the tower to see if they have met the challenge.

ROUND 4

The judge stands high up again and reads out Genesis 11:8,9. He or she should congratulate your group members if the tower has reached the target. Then send them off in teams as far away as possible from each other – as long as they can still hear you!

Say: *God judged the people for going their own way and ignoring him. They wanted to make a name for themselves rather than recognizing that God was the best. He decided what was right and wrong – only he could. People who did wrong wouldn't get away with it for ever. They brought suffering on themselves and on the world. They still do.*

  10

SCOREBOARD

Display the Theme Scoreboard. In their teams, get the group members to discuss whether any of the themes appeared in the Bible verses the judge read. Hand out felt-tip pens to five confident writers. Invite each team to say where it spotted the themes. Ask the writers to note them on the appropriate part of the Scoreboard each time. Add any thoughts you had during 'Your own time with God'.

  5

SPACE

Rather than standing tall, get your group members to lie flat on their backs with their eyes closed. Encourage them to picture in their minds some of the things that are wrong with the world. Pause, then lead them in this response, but only if they can mean what you're asking them to say:

Leader: Lord,
Group members: We're really sorry.

Then ask them to think of anything in themselves that they know doesn't please God and to tell him secretly about it. Pause, then lead them in the same response again.

Finish by doing the 'Civilization?' **Shout** together.

LEADER: LORD

GROUP MEMBERS: WE'RE REALLY SORRY

GRUNT'N'STUFF CARDS

CIVILIZATION?

GOD'S WAY'S BEST,
DON'T CHOOSE WHAT'S WRONG.
WRONG MIGHT SEEM GOOD,
BUT IT WON'T LAST LONG.

3 GOING PLACES

ABRAHAM

AIMS
To help group members:
- grasp that God makes promises he will keep
- see that it's OK to risk everything for God

SCOPE
Through Abraham's life God demonstrated his determination to make a new start in overcoming wrong and in creating his own people. God enabled Abraham to enjoy a close relationship with him: a model of what he wanted for all people.

BIBLE BASE
Genesis 12:1–9; Hebrews 11:8–12

MATERIALS AND EQUIPMENT
Have one of each of the following for each team of players:
- a Bible
- a 'Going places' Game Map, Game Card and a set of Clue Cards (pages 21, 22 and 23)
- a set of Promise Shapes (page 24)
- a set of Serious Hazard Cards (page 24)
- a reel of sticky tape
- a pen

For your own preparation and for other parts of the session, you'll need:
- your copy of the Leader Theme Card (page 7) and Bible
- an overhead projector and screen (optional)
- background music on tape or CD
- a tape or CD player
- a good handful of sand
- beachwear for one person (shorts, sandals, T-shirt, towel, sun cream, hat, sunglasses, etc)
- a small prize
- large place names – 'Ur', 'Haran', 'Shechem', 'Bethel/Ai', 'Egypt', 'Hebron'
- a set of Clue Cards (page 23)
- fine shingle/tiny stones
- a shoebox or similar
- Blu-tack
- thick felt-tip pens
- a midwife's uniform and gear
- a new-born baby (surely someone could lend you one?!)
- the Theme Scoreboard
- an enlarged version of the session **Symbol** and **Shout** (page 25) on an overhead projector acetate or paper

PREPARATION

DO 'YOUR OWN TIME WITH GOD' (SEE BELOW). FAMILIARISE YOURSELF WITH THE SESSION OUTLINE. GET TOGETHER ALL THE MATERIALS AND EQUIPMENT YOU NEED.

YOUR OWN TIME WITH GOD
In an 'instant' world of short-term gains, the story of Abraham encourages us to live by faith in the long-term, broad-canvas God. He wants us to look for gain in heaven. Try to imagine yourself as Abraham hearing God's words in Genesis 12:1–9. Promises of land, descendants, and that somehow Abraham's life would eventually bring good to every nation in the world must have been pretty mind-boggling for him!

READ GENESIS 12:1–9 HEBREWS 11:8–12

God made many promises with the words 'I will…'. Abraham's part was to step into the unknown. Read in Hebrews 11:8–12 how his life was later interpreted. Pray that your group members will want either to take a deep breath and trust in our faithful God for the first time, or be even more confident in him now.

2000 BC › 1900 BC › 180 BC › 1700 BC

BIBLE EVENTS
All dates approximate

1900 BC Abram and his family leave Haran to travel to Canaan.

OTHER WORLD EVENTS

2000 BC The Bronze Age begins in Europe. The earliest Minoan palace is built at Knossos, Crete.

1925 BC The Hittites conquer Babylon.

1900 BC The Amorites overthrow the Sumerian civilizations of Ur and dominate Mesopotamia.

1830 BC The Babylonians rule Assyria (until 1810 BC).

1800 BC Babylon conquers the city states of northern and southern Mesopotamia.
King Hammurabi publishes his 'Eye for an eye' law code, the first legal system.

1750 BC The Hyksos (nomads from Syria and Palestine) invade Egypt.

1700 BC The Hittites cross Turkey into Syria.

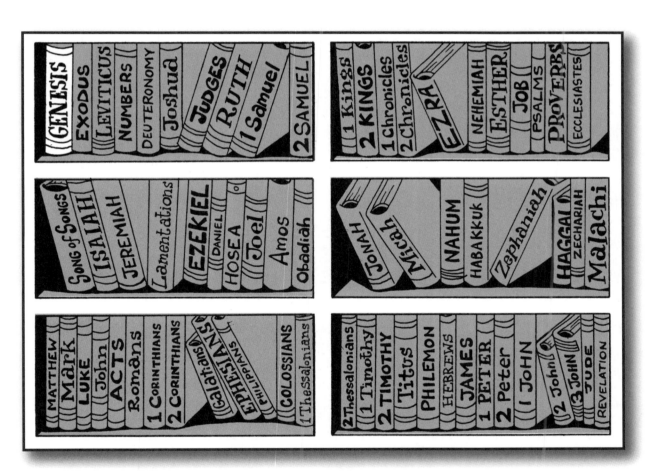

HANDY HINT
If you're feeling really adventurous, make up a Bible 'library' from empty DVD cases – one DVD case for each Bible book. You'll need 66, so see if you can do a deal with your local DVD hire shop.

Make your own Bible book covers and place them as the DVD fly sheet. Colour-code the covers of each type of book – history, prophecy, Gospel, etc. You could then build up the 'library' session by session as you work through *Absolutely Everything!* You may even be able to encourage your group to learn the order of the Bible books by heart.

3 GOING PLACES

Have one leader dressed in jazzy beach gear.

SCENE-SETTER

Your beach bather should grab a handful of sand and offer a prize for the closest guess as to how many grains he or she is holding (around 4,500,000 grains if his or her hand is the same size as mine). Ask the group to imagine how many grains there would be on a whole beach! God told one man that he would have as many descendants as that (though obviously we're talking mind-blowing pictures here, not exact numbers).

Introduce the **Scheme** along these lines: *The word 'Genesis' means beginnings.* (Ask for a few suggestions of what beginnings they have seen in the last two sessions.) *With so much wrong happening around the place, God wanted the whole world back on his side. He had a plan. He chose one tiny man in one tiny part of the world. But he made him a HUGE promise.* (Get someone to read out Genesis 22:17,18.) *Now imagine you're Abraham. You've got a lot of life to live in just a few minutes!*

SYMBOL AND SHOUT

Repeat the **Shout** together (page 25) until everyone can say it by heart. Keep the **Shout** and **Symbol** visible for the whole session.

SCHEME

Display the place names: Haran, Ur, Shechem, Bethel/Ai, Hebron, Egypt. Near each, put the appropriate Clue Card (page 23). Place a box near you, at a central location. It should contain the following items (a complete set for each team):

• Promise Shapes: 1 (crowd), 2 (land), 3 (dust), 4 (star)
• Serious Hazard Cards 1–4
• two tiny stones

Play in teams of two or three with at least one strong reader in each team. Give each team a Bible, a 'Going places' Map, a Game Card, a pen and sticky tape. The teams begin at Ur. At each place they visit, they must work through the Clue Card, checking the Bible verses, answering the questions and completing the tasks. The last item on each Clue Card gives the next place to go to. Stagger the start so the teams don't all arrive at the same place at the same time or copy others.

At the end, get someone to read out Genesis 21:1–8. He or she could dress up in a midwife's gear carrying a new-born baby in one arm and a Bible in the opposite hand. Isaac's birth was the physical proof that God's promise to Abraham and Sarah would come true. Abraham's 'descendants' started with him.

SCOREBOARD

Work at the Theme Scoreboard all together. Do the usual writing up, adding any thoughts from 'Your own time with God'.

SPACE

Put on quiet background music. Encourage the group members to ignore each other as they walk 50 paces around the room, looking down at their feet. They should then stop, sit on the floor and silently thank God for the good things he has done for them. Ask them to get up, walk another 50 paces, sit down and tell God how committed they are to going his way. (Maybe not at all?) At the next stop they should thank God for any of his promises they can remember from the Bible. Add more 'prayer stops' if you like, giving clear instructions each time.

Finish by letting rip with the 'Going places' **Shout**.

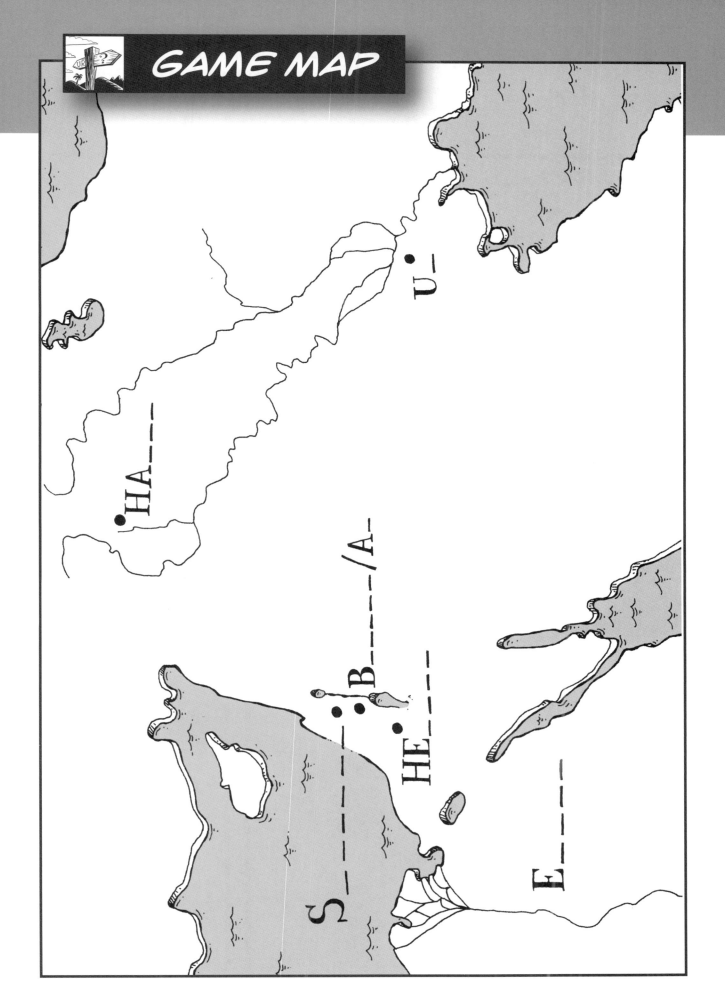

GAME CARD

....

....

PLACE 1

1
....
2
....
3
....

PLACE 2

2
....
3
....
5
....
6
....

PLACE 3

2
....
4
....
5
....

PLACE 4

2
....
4
....

Don't fill in any more until
you get back here!
5
....
7
....
9
....

PLACE 5

2
....
4
....
5
....
6
....

PLACE 6

2
....
4
....
6
....

CLUE CARDS

CARD 1   UR

The start of the journey
Read out the Bible verses to the whole team and work on the answers together.

1 What happy event for Abram took place in Ur? Genesis 11:27–30
2 Who told who to do what? Acts 7:2,3
3 Where did Abram head for next? Acts 7:4 (first part)

Well, go there then, as quickly as you can!

CARD 4   BETHEL / AI

Read out the Bible verses to the whole team and work on the answers together.

1 On your map, draw in Abram's route so far. Name the places.
2 What did Abram build between Bethel and Ai? Genesis 12:8 (second part). (Grab a small stone and stick it in the 'Bethel/Ai' box.)
3 Collect Serious Hazard Card 1, read it out and stick it in the box.
4 So where did Abram head for next? Genesis 12:10

Now move those legs!

WARNING! Only do questions 5 to 9 when you come back here again!

5 Remember, Lot was Abram's nephew. What was the problem between them? Genesis 13:5,6
6 Collect Serious Hazard Card 3, read it out and stick it in the box.
7 What was Abram's solution to the problem? Genesis 13:8,9
8 Pick up Promise Shape 3, read it out and stick it in the box.
9 Where did Abram head for next? Genesis 13:18 (first part)

Well, move camp then!

CARD 5   EGYPT

Read out the Bible verses to the whole team and work on the answers together.

1 On your map, draw in Abram's route so far. Name the places.
2 What was Abram afraid of? Genesis 12:11–13
3 Collect Serious Hazard Card 2, read it out and stick it in the 'Egypt' box on your sheet.
4 What happened to the king when he grabbed Sarai for himself? Genesis 12:17
5 So what did the king do to Abram and Sarai? Genesis 12:18–20
6 Where did they head for next? Genesis 13:1–4

Go back there then and do the second lot of clues!

CARD 2   HARAN

Read out the Bible verses to the whole team and work on the answers together.

1 On your map, draw in Abram's route so far. Name the places.
2 What sad event happened in Haran? Genesis 11:31,32
3 Who told who to do what? Genesis 12:1
4 Collect Promise Shape 1, read it aloud and stick it in the 'Haran' box on your answer sheet.
5 Where should Abram and his family head for next? Genesis 12:4,5
6 At which town did they arrive? (The sacred tree of Moreh was there.) Genesis 12:6

Well, get a move on then – go there!

CARD 3   SCHECHEM

Read out the Bible verses to the whole team and work on the answers together.

1 On your map, draw in Abram's route so far. Name the places.
2 Who made an appearance to Abram at Shechem? Genesis 12:7
3 Pick up Promise Shape 2, read it aloud and tick it in the 'Shechem' box on your answer sheet.
4 What did Abram build? Genesis 12:7 (Grab a small stone and stick it in the 'Shechem' box.)
5 Where did Abram head for next? Genesis 12:8 (first part)

OK, what are you waiting for?

CARD 6   HEBRON

Read out the Bible verses to the whole team and work on the answers together.

1 On your map, draw in Abram's route so far. Name the places.
2 What construction work did Abram do at Hebron? Genesis 13:18 (second part) (Collect a small stone and stick it in the 'Hebron' box on your sheet.)
3 Pick up Serious Hazard Card 4, read it out and stick it in the box.
4 What was Abram bothered about? Genesis 15:1–3
5 Collect Promise Shape 4, read it out and stick it in the box.
6 What's the best thing that could be said about Abram? Genesis 15:6

Now get your answer sheet and map back to your leader fast!

Photocopy and cut out these Promise Shapes and Serious Hazard Cards for use with the Game Card on page 22.

PROMISE SHAPES

PROMISE 1

GENESIS 12:2,3

God said, 'I will bless you and make your descendants into a great nation. You will become famous and be a blessing to others. I will bless anyone who blesses you, but I will put a curse on anyone who puts a curse on you. Everyone on earth will be blessed because of you.'

PROMISE 3

GENESIS 13:14–17

God said, 'Look around to the north, south, east and west. I will give you and your family all the land you can see. It will be theirs for ever! I will give you more descendants than there are specks of dust on the earth; it will be easier to count the specks of dust than to count your descendants. Now walk back and forth across the land, because I am giving it to you.'

PROMISE 2

GENESIS 12:7

God said, 'I will give this land to your family for ever.'

PROMISE 4

GENESIS 15:5

God said, 'Look at the sky and see if you can count the stars. That's how many descendants you will have.'

SERIOUS HAZARD CARDS

SERIOUS HAZARD 1

GENESIS 12:10

Famine in Canaan. Abram moved to Egypt.

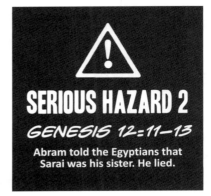

SERIOUS HAZARD 2

GENESIS 12:11–13

Abram told the Egyptians that Sarai was his sister. He lied.

SERIOUS HAZARD 3

GENESIS 13:7

Quarrels between Abram's and Lot's men because there wasn't enough pasture for their herds.

SERIOUS HAZARD 4

GENESIS 14:1–16

Lot and all his possessions captured by hostile kings. Abram risked his life to rescue Lot and all his stuff.

GOING PLACES

TO WIN THE WORLD BACK
GOD HAS A GREAT PLAN.
JUST TRUST WHAT HE SAYS,
DON'T DOUBT THAT HE CAN.

4 FREE AT LAST!

THE EXODUS AND THE TEN COMMANDMENTS

AIMS
To help group members:
- look for the five key themes in the Exodus and in the giving of the Ten Commandments
- realise that to live to please God is true freedom

SCOPE
After years of slavery in Egypt, God set the Israelites free and gave them the Ten Commandments and other rules. They were his special, 'redeemed' people, so God expected them to worship and obey him. He wanted to protect them and to show them the best way to live.

BIBLE BASE
Exodus 19:4–6; 19:16 – 20:21; Romans 6:15–23

MATERIALS AND EQUIPMENT
Each pair or three will need:
- a Bible
- a set of 16 'Free at last!' Game Cards (page 30, enlarged to A3 size and cut up)
- a pen
- a sheet of paper

For your own preparation and for other parts of the session, you'll need:
- your copy of the Leader Theme Card (page 7) and Bible
- two or three inflated balloons
- a cheap and cheerful prize
- a firefighter's outfit or a uniform of one of the emergency services
- an overhead projector and screen (optional)
- Exodus 3:7,8 on an overhead projector acetate or large sheet of paper
- thick felt-tip pens
- the Theme Scoreboard
- an enlarged version of the session **Symbol** and **Shout** (page 31) on overhead projector acetate or paper

PREPARATION

DO 'YOUR OWN TIME WITH GOD' (SEE BELOW). REMEMBER TO PRAY FOR YOUR GROUP MEMBERS INDIVIDUALLY BY NAME. FAMILIARISE YOURSELF WITH THE SESSION OUTLINE. GET TOGETHER ALL THE MATERIALS AND EQUIPMENT YOU NEED.

YOUR OWN TIME WITH GOD
Remind yourself of God's promises to Abram in Genesis 12:1–3 and 15:12–16. In this session we see these promises beginning to be fulfilled as the Israelites become slaves in Egypt, are rescued, and are then given the Ten Commandments by God. God never intended the Ten Commandments and other laws to be another kind of slavery for his people, but a pathway to freedom. The laws were boundaries within which they could live life to the full, in a safe, God-devoted, God-glorifying way. Notice that God gave the laws after he had reminded Moses of his love, of the 'covenant' and of the huge privileges attached to being his special people. He also filled the sky with a spectacular reminder of who he was. Enjoy Exodus 19:4–6, then 19:16 – 20:21. Don't forget to use your Leader Theme Card.

READ
EXODUS 19:4–6;
19:16 – 20:21;
ROMANS 6:15–23

Stimulated by Romans 6:15–23, once again thank God for Jesus who sets us free from the 'slavery of sin' if we ask him. Use some phrases from the verses in your prayer if you like. Now pray that your group members will be excited about the freedom of living to please God and will not think it a drag. In this session there's a whole lot about God creating, saving, promising, and showing who he is, as well as judging!

| 1300 BC | 1250 BC | 1200 BC | |

BIBLE EVENTS

All dates approximate

1250 BC   God rescued the Israelites from slavery in Egypt – the Exodus – and led them through the desert, via Mount Sinai, to the east side of the Jordan.

OTHER WORLD EVENTS

1300 BC   The Medes and Persians move into Iran.

1292–1225 BC   Rameses II rules Egypt, extending his empire into Asia. The temples of Abu Simbel are constructed.

1200 BC   The 'Peoples of the Sea' devastate Syria and Palestine, but are beaten back from Egypt by Rameses III; some of the survivors settle on the coast of Palestine under the name of 'Philistines'.

11193 BC   The Greeks destroy Troy and end the ten–year Trojan War.

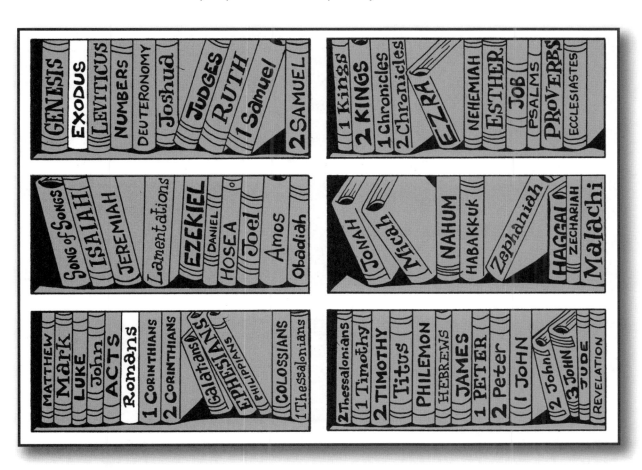

HANDY HINT

This age group seems more and more inclined to 'switch off' as soon as anyone starts talking to them from the front in a group session. So cultivate the habit of expecting their attention and keeping it. When you do the small bits of straight talk (either the storyline or explanations of an activity), gather your group members round you as close as possible and maintain eye contact with them. Don't let anyone sit or stand behind you.

4 FREE AT LAST!

> **READ**
> EXODUS 3:7,8

Get one leader to dress as a firefighter or someone else who rescues and shows the way out of danger. This character should simply join in with the session and see if any group members can make the connection with Moses. (Tenuous maybe, but unforgettable!)

  10 ⏱

SCENE-SETTER

Divide your group into two teams, ideally with an adult cheerleader for each. Get everyone excited about playing 'Balloon Anarchy' but don't tell them the rules. Say that the aim is to keep the balloon off the ground. Throw up a balloon between the two teams and shout 'Go!' Keep stopping the game for infringements of rules which you make up as you go along, eg heading, jumping, laughing. The first person to ask 'What are the rules?' gets the prize.

@ 🔊 5 ⏱

SYMBOL AND SHOUT

Display the 'Free at last!' **Symbol** and **Shout** (page 31). Keep them visible for the rest of the session. Divide your group into teams of two or three, making sure that there is at least one strong reader in each. Get them to teach each other the **Shout** by heart in three minutes flat. Hear each team chant it before moving on to the **Scheme**.

Introduce the **Scheme** in this way:
Abraham (remember him?) died at the age of 175. Now, his grandson Jacob had 12 sons – Reuben, Simeon, Levi, Judah, Zebulun, Issachar, Dan, Gad, Asher, Naphtali, Joseph and Benjamin. Jacob's large family went to Egypt and ended up staying. For 400 years. Surprise, surprise – Reuben, Simeon and the rest didn't last that long. But, in 400 years, 12 brothers

could have a lot of children who could have a lot of children who could have a lot of children. Jacob and his sons had turned into a whole race of people, the Israelites. (Israel was another name for Jacob.) The Egyptian king was worried. He made them slaves to stop them taking over! But, in the Bible book of Exodus, God promised the Israelites... (Show and read out Exodus 3:7,8.) And that's exactly what he did. God sent horrible plagues to help the Egyptian king make up his mind to let the Israelites go. The Israelites' rescue and departure from Egypt led by Moses is called the 'Exodus', the 'way out'. They were God's people and, on the way to the land he had promised them, God told them exactly how he wanted them to live.

 25 ⏱

SCHEME

Give each team of two or three group members a Bible, a set of 16 'Free at last!' Game Cards (copied and cut up from page 30), a pen and a sheet of paper.

Each team should place their 16 cards face up in front of them. There are nine rounds to this game. Lead the teams through the game a round at a time. Issue the challenges, allow time for the teams to react, then check everyone's answer. Trust teams not to look at what others are doing and to keep their own scores on their sheets of paper.

ROUND 1

Pick out a card which gives the very good reason why God gave his people the Ten Commandments.
Answer: 'God loved the people of Israel so much that he wanted them to be dedicated to him alone and to be safe and secure. They had to show the rest of the world what God was like by the way they lived.'
Score: 3 points for the correct card.

ROUND 2

Tear up the not-the-reason why God gave his people the Ten Commandments.
Answer: 'God didn't like the people of Israel that much and wanted to make life as hard as possible for them.'
Score: 2 points for the correct card.

ROUND 3

Scrunch up and throw as far as you can the two rules that you think don't appear in the Ten Commandments.
Answer: 'Never carry more than three donkeys – you'll kill yourself!' and 'Pound strangers to dust if they come anywhere near your tent.'
Score: 1 point for each correct card.

ROUND 4

Use a Bible to sort the commandments into the order in which they appear in Exodus 20.
Answer: Check out Exodus 20:3–17.
Score: 2 bonus points – not much brain work was needed there!

Now get everyone to try to memorise the order they are in without writing anything down. Explain that they'll need to get them back in this order later without looking at a Bible.

ROUND 5

Sort the commandments into three piles: those that are about people's relationship with God, those that are about people's relationships with other people, and the one that is about both.
Answer: About their relationship with God (Exodus 20:3–7); about other people (vs 12–17); about both (vs 8–11).
Score: 1 point for each correctly placed commandment.

ROUND 6

The Ten Commandments were for the good of God's people for all time, but different generations are mentioned in different commandments. Pick out any commandments that mention the last generation or future generations.
Answer: Last generation in verse 12; future generations in verses 4–6.
Score: 2 points for each correctly chosen commandment.

ROUND 7

The Ten Commandments tell us a lot about who God is and what he is like. Use your cards (including the blanks) to create the word 'God' in capital letters. No tearing, cutting or bending!
Score: 5 points for managing the task successfully.

ROUND 8

Lay out 12 cards to make a 'safety fence' around a square area of floor. The cards must be touching. The first team to have two people standing safely inside the 'fence' without touching the sides will get five bonus points. The Ten Commandments and other laws provided the boundaries beyond which God's people should not go.
Score: 5 bonus points for the first team.

ROUND 9

Put the Ten Commandments back into the right order, without looking at a Bible.
Score: 2 points for each correctly placed commandment.

SCOREBOARD

Focus on the Theme Scoreboard. Get each pair or three to list where any of the five themes appear in the Exodus and the giving of the Ten Commandments. Ask the teams to read out their lists in turn. Carefully question any answers that don't seem to tie in with what the Bible says. When any team hears something mentioned which is also on their list, they must cross it off. At the end invite each team to graffiti the items left on their list onto the Scoreboard. As you go along, also feed in any insights from 'Your own time with God'.

SPACE

We can now have a good relationship with God not by trying to be good and to keep the rules but by trusting in Jesus. Allow space for everyone to ask God to forgive them for anything they have done recently that hasn't pleased him.

Finish by bellowing out the 'Free at last!' **Shout** together.

GAME CARDS

Do not **WORSHIP** any god except me.

RESPECT your father and your mother, and you will live a long time in the land I am giving you.

DO NOT misuse my name. I am the Lord your God, and I will punish anyone who misuses my name.

Do not **MAKE** idols that look like anything in the sky or on the earth or in the sea under the earth. Don't bow down and worship idols. I am the Lord your God, and I demand all your love. If you reject me, I will punish your families for three or four generations. But if you love me and obey my laws, I will be kind to your families for thousands of generations.

Do not **MURDER**.

God didn't **LIKE** the people of Israel that much and wanted to make life as hard as possible for them.

Be **FAITHFUL** in marriage.

Never **CARRY** more than three donkeys – you'll kill yourself!

Do not **STEAL**.

Do not **WANT** to take anything that belongs to someone else. Don't want to take anyone's house, wife or husband, slaves, oxen, donkeys or anything else.

Do not tell **LIES** about others.

REMEMBER that the Sabbath day belongs to me. You have six days when you can do your work, but the seventh day of each week belongs to me, your God. No one is to work on that day – not you, your children, your slaves, your animals, or the foreigners who live in your towns. In six days I made the sky, the earth, the seas, and everything in them, but on the seventh day I rested. That's why I made the Sabbath a special day that belongs to me.

God **LOVED** the people of Israel so much that he wanted them to be dedicated to him alone and to be safe and secure. They had to show the rest of the world what God was like by the way they lived.

POUND strangers to dust if they come anywhere near your tent.

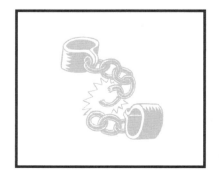

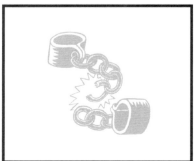

30

FREE
AT LAST!

IF YOU WANT TO BE FREE,
JUST LOVE THE BIG G.
THEN MAKE SURE YOU STAY TRUE
TO WHAT HE WANTS YOU TO DO.

5 TRIBAL RIVALS

TRIBES, JUDGES AND KINGS — LIFE IN THE PROMISED LAND

AIMS
To help group members:
- **understand the struggles and distractions of life for God's people in Canaan**
- **grasp that God remains faithful even though people disappoint him.**

SCOPE
After years of wandering in the wilderness, much of it caused by their own disobedience to God, the people of Israel finally arrived in Canaan. But life in their Promised Land was not all ease and comfort. First they had to fight their way in against the peoples who already lived there, then they were constantly under attack from surrounding tribes. Later they got into serious trouble caused by kings who didn't obey God.

BIBLE BASE
Joshua 3; Judges 2:1–19; 1 Samuel 8:4–21; Hebrews 11:32–40

MATERIALS AND EQUIPMENT
Each team will need:
- a Game Map cut into pieces like a jigsaw (page 36)
- a Judges Cycle Sheet (page 37)
- a pen
- Kings and Queen Sheets (pages 38,39) cut up into individual cards
- a Bible for each person

For your own preparation and for other parts of the session, you'll need:
- your copy of the Leader Theme Card (page 7) and Bible
- an overhead projector and screen (optional)
- newspapers or magazines for 'Snowballs'
- a copy of the Game Map (page 36) on acetate or enlarged to A3 on paper
- an army general's uniform, genuine or improvised (optional)
- Isaiah 9:6,7 on an overhead projector acetate or large sheet of paper
- thick felt-tip pens
- small Post-it notes
- background music on CD
- a CD player
- an enlarged version of the session **Symbol** and **Shout** (page 40) on an overhead projector acetate or paper
- the Theme Scoreboard

PREPARATION

DO 'YOUR OWN TIME WITH GOD' (SEE BELOW). GET USED TO THE FLOW OF THE SESSION BECAUSE IT'S SLIGHTLY TRICKIER THAN USUAL. GET TOGETHER ALL THE MATERIALS AND EQUIPMENT YOU NEED.

YOUR OWN TIME WITH GOD
Begin by talking with God about your future. What are your plans? Do things look bright or gloomy? Which of God's promises help you most when thinking about the future? Read Judges 2:1–19, noting on your Leader Theme Card any glimpses of the five themes.

Through this period of history, things usually looked a mess. God's people often forgot about him and disobeyed him. Occasionally a king or other leader shone out as someone devoted to God and determined to help the people live God's way. However, through it all God remained faithful and had a plan for his people that was even better than reaching Canaan. Soak in Hebrews 11:32–40, especially the last two verses. Pray that, through this session, your group members will be overwhelmed by God's love and faithfulness.

READ
JOSHUA 3;
JUDGES 2:1–19;
1 SAMUEL 8:4–21;
HEBREWS 11:32–40

| 1200 BC | 1100 BC | 1000 BC | 900 BC | 800 BC |

BIBLE EVENTS

All dates approximate

1200 BC The Israelites enter Canaan.

1020 BC Samuel anoints Saul king of the Israelites.

1000 BC David (King of Judah then of Israel, too) makes Jerusalem his capital and brings the ark of the covenant (containing the Ten Commandments) to the city.

960 BC King David is succeeded by Solomon who builds the first temple in Jerusalem.

933 BC Solomon's kingdom is divided between his son Rehoboam and a court official Jeroboam. The land is divided in two – Judah and Israel.

OTHER WORLD EVENTS

1200 BC The 'Peoples of the Sea' devastate Syria and Palestine, but are beaten back from Egypt by Rameses III; some of the survivors settle on the coast of Palestine under the name of 'Philistines'.

1150 BC The Mycenaean power collapses.

1125 BC Nebuchadnezzar I beats back Assyrian invasion of Babylon.

1000 BC Iron tools are made in the Ganges Valley in India. The Etruscans – a race with a unique language and religion – inhabit upper Italy.

935 BC Bring on the first great period of the new Assyrian Empire!

814 BC The Phoenicians establish Carthage in North Africa.

800 BC Homer composes the Iliad and Odyssey at about this time.

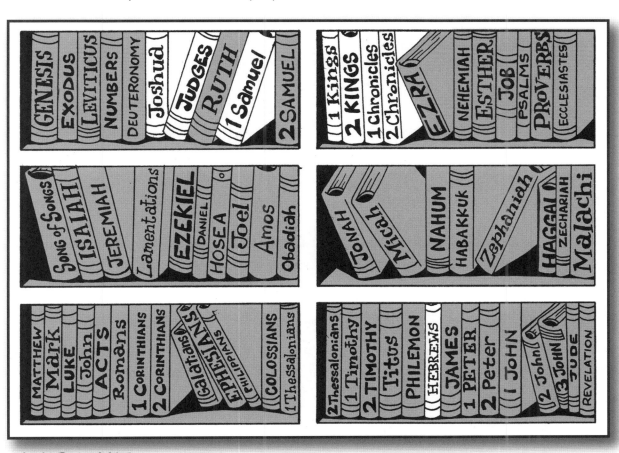

HANDY HINT

Absolutely Everything! works on the principle that your group members will be heavily involved in the learning all through the session. Every part of it is designed to draw them into it enthusiastically. However, watch for any group members who sit back and let others do the work. Encourage them to get stuck in and make the experience good for everyone. They have a vital part to play.

5 TRIBAL RIVALS

> **READ**
> EXODUS 3:7,8

**Have a leader dressed as a general throughout this session.
He or she could keep discipline in the ranks!**

 10

SCENE-SETTER

Play 'Snowballs'. Split your group into two teams of equal numbers. Divide the two teams by a row of chairs. Give the teams identical amounts of paper – three newspapers or magazines for each. On the word 'Go!' they must roll sheets of paper up like snowballs and throw them over the chair divide. The winning team is the one with the least amount of paper on its side after four minutes.

@ 5

SYMBOL AND SHOUT

Display the 'Tribal rivals' **Symbol** and **Shout** (page 40). Learn the **Shout** by heart together, and keep both **Symbol** and **Shout** visible throughout the session.

Introduce the **Scheme** by saying something like this: *After God had got the Israelites out of Egypt they spent 40 years living in the desert. In the end Joshua led the Israelites into Canaan: the land God had promised them. They won lots of battles against the people who were already living there, starting with the city of Jericho. Then they divided the land among their tribes and settled down. But life for God's people wasn't very settled or easy.*

◎ 25

SCHEME

Divide your group into teams of up to four players. They are about to experience the 'Colossal Canaan Challenge', a game in three rounds. Since there is a lot of history to cover in this session, there will be more leader input than usual, but hopefully the session will still move along in a lively way.

ROUND 1	Hand a set of Game Map cut-up jigsaw pieces (page 36) to each team. On the word 'Go!' they have two minutes to try to settle the tribes of Israel into the Promised Land by piecing the jigsaw together. If you want the game to be competitive, award three points to any team that achieves it within the time limit. Show your correct version of the map so that everyone can check they have it right before you move on. All teams should keep their map intact.

Offer a bonus point for any team that can give one of the two answers to the question: Which two of Jacob's sons do not have their name on the map as a tribe? The answers are 'Levi' and 'Joseph'. Explain that the tribe of Levi didn't get a portion of land because God chose them to be priests for all the rest. So they lived among the other tribes. Joseph is represented by Manasseh and Ephraim, his two sons.

Now tell everyone to listen to what General Joshua had warned God's people just before he died. The leader who is dressed as the army general should leap up and read Joshua 23:3–7 in an authoritarian voice.

Introduce Round 2 in this way: *Of course the peoples who were already living in Canaan weren't going to sit there and let their land be taken over. Tribes like the Philistines, Ammonites, Moabites and Edomites caused God's people huge trouble. But God sent the Israelites 'judges' to defend them. Judges were superheroes, not people in courts with funny wigs. Many of them were brilliant army commanders.*

Give out Bibles to everyone and get them to flick through the book of Judges, finding and shouting out some of the judges' names in the headings.

Hand each team a Judges Cycle Sheet (page 37) and a pen. Challenge them to write on the sheet what kept happening to God's people at the time of the judges. Full instructions are on the sheet. Allow **7 minutes only** for them to complete the sheet. Award three points for the first team and one point for any other team that gets the right answer within the time limit.

Introduce Round 3 in this way: *The last judge was Samuel, not a soldier but a prophet, someone who told the people what God wanted them to know. Now the Israelites wanted a king like all the other peoples around them. Samuel advised them against having a human ruler, but God let them learn the hard way and appointed Saul as king. Saul disobeyed God. But he was followed by two great kings: David and then his son, Solomon. After Solomon died, the nation split apart. The tribes of Judah and Benjamin (and probably some of Simeon's lot) in the south, stayed faithful to Solomon's son Rehoboam. The other tribes wanted Jeroboam as king. After this, the bit in the south was called Judah, and the bit in the north Israel.*

Get each team to split their map into two across the appropriate line (see page 36).

From then on there was a mix of rulers in Judah and Israel who either followed God or didn't.

Give each team a copy of the Kings and Queen Sheets (pages 38,39) cut into individual cards. Each team has to divide the cards into two sets: 'Kings of Israel' and 'Kings and Queen of Judah'. This is shown on the cards. They must then use Bibles to further divide them into those who generally obeyed God and those who mostly disobeyed him. They can also have a 'Don't know' column. Allow **7 minutes only** for them to do this, working as a team in the most effective way.

If you want to, award three points to the first team to complete the sorting correctly. Give one point to every other team that gets it right. The layout on pages 38 and 39 shows the correct answers.

Say: *Amazingly few rulers pleased God – and these were supposed to be people who belonged to him! But the good news is that God never gave up on his people but promised them that one day they would have the best king ever. Show Isaiah 9:6,7 and read it out.*

READ
JOSHUA 23:3—7
ISAIAH 9:6,7

SCOREBOARD

In the same teams, get everyone to discuss where they noticed any of the themes in today's session.

Listen to the feedback from each team and ask for two volunteers to add to the Theme Scoreboard your summary of what the teams have said.

SPACE

Sitting round the Scoreboard, invite group members to pray out loud or silently. Either they can thank God for something they have discovered about him or they can ask for practical help to live as his people in their homes and schools. They might pray from a comment that was written on a poster in an earlier session – that doesn't matter. Give everyone a small Post-it note and, as you play background music, get them to stick their Post-it by the theme comment that they have been praying about. This in itself could be an important act of prayer.

Finish by doing the 'Tribal rivals' **Shout** together.

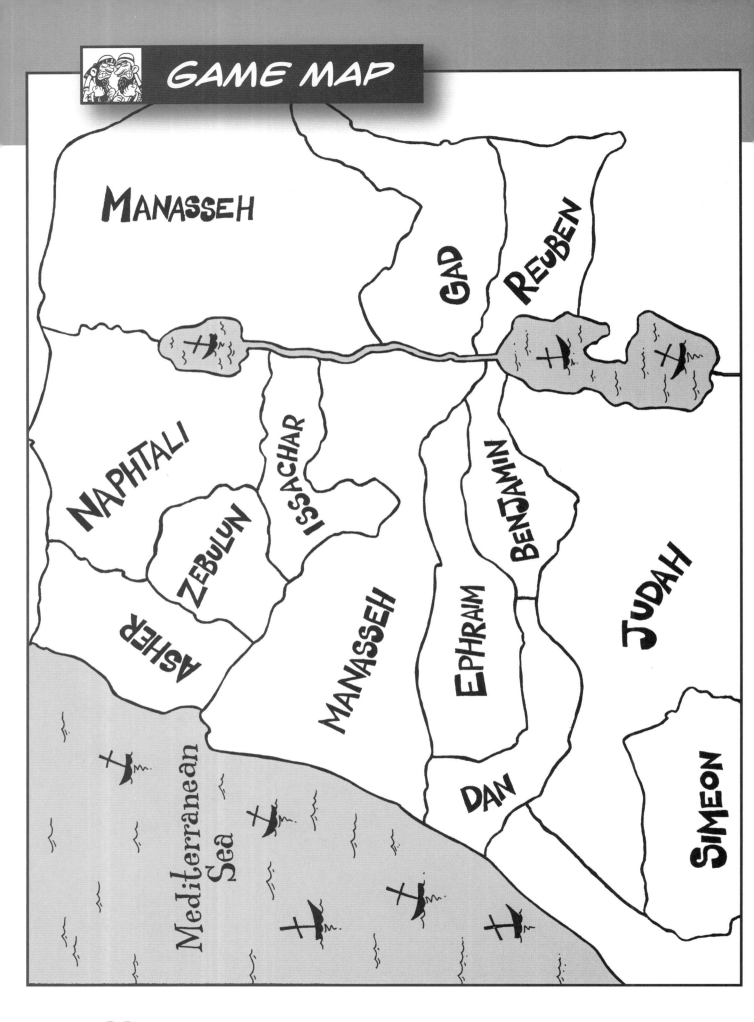

JUDGES CYCLE

INSTRUCTIONS

- Look up the story of judge Othniel in Judges 3:7–11.
- Get one of your team to read it out.
- Write in the boxes 1 to 4 what happened.
- Now check that what you have written is true for all the judges. Get everyone to glance at the story of judge Jephthah in Judges 10:6–18 and 11:29–33.
- Wave to your group leader if you're satisfied that what you have written on your sheet is true for all the judges.

1 THE ISRAELITES

5 SILENCE...

2 THEIR ENEMIES

4 GOD

Just before he died, Joshua reminded the people of Judah, 'The Lord is our God. He gave us this wonderful land and made an agreement with us that we would worship only him. But if you worship other gods, it will make the Lord furious. He will start getting rid of you, and soon not one of you will be left in this good land that he has given you.'

3 THE ISRAELITES

KINGS AND QUEENS OF JUDAH

MOSTLY OBEYED GOD ▽	**UZZIAH** KING OF JUDAH 767–740 BC 2 Kings 15:1–3	**JEHORAM** KING OF JUDAH 848–841 BC 2 Kings 8:16–19	**AHAZIAH** KING OF JUDAH 841 BC 2 Kings 8:25–27
	JOTHAM KING OF JUDAH 740–732 BC 2 Kings 15:32–34	**ATHALIAH** QUEEN OF JUDAH 841–835 BC 2 Chronicles 24:7	**AHAZ** KING OF JUDAH 732–716 BC 2 Kings 16:1,2
ASA KING OF JUDAH 911–870 BC 1 Kings 15:9–11	**HEZEKIAH** KING OF JUDAH 716–687 BC 2 Kings 18:1–3	**MANASSEH** KING OF JUDAH 687–643 BC 2 Kings 21:1,2	**AMON** KING OF JUDAH 643–641 BC 2 Kings 21:19–22
JEHOSHAPHAT KING OF JUDAH 870–848 BC 1 Kings 22:41–43	**JOSIAH** KING OF JUDAH 640–609 BC 2 Kings 22:1,2	**JEHOAHAZ** KING OF JUDAH 609 BC 2 Kings 23:31,32	**JEHOIAKIM** KING OF JUDAH 609–597 BC 2 Kings 23:35–37
JOASH KING OF JUDAH 835–796 BC 2 Kings 12:1–3	**MOSTLY DISOBEYED GOD** ▽	**JEHOIACHIN** KING OF JUDAH 597 BC 2 Kings 24:8,9	**ZEDEKIAH** KING OF JUDAH 597–587 BC 2 Kings 24:18–20
AMAZIAH KING OF JUDAH 796–767 BC 2 Kings 14:1–4	**REHOBOAM** KING OF JUDAH 931 BC 2 Chronicles 12:13,14	**ABIJAH** KING OF JUDAH 913–911 BC 1 Kings 15:1–3	**DON'T KNOW!** ▽

KINGS OF ISRAEL

ZIMRI
KING OF ISRAEL
885 BC
1 Kings 16:17–19

HOSHEA
KING OF ISRAEL
732–723 BC
2 Kings 17:1,2

JEROBOAM II
KING OF ISRAEL
782–753 BC
2 Kings 14:23,24

MOSTLY OBEYED GOD

AHAB
KING OF ISRAEL
874–853 BC
1 Kings 16:30,31

NADAB
KING OF ISRAEL
910–909 BC
1 Kings 15:25,26

MENAHEM
KING OF ISRAEL
752–742 BC
2 Kings 15:17,18

JEHU
KING OF ISRAEL
841–814 BC
2 Kings 10:28–31

JEHORAM
KING OF ISRAEL
852–841 BC
2 Kings 3:1–3

ELAH
KING OF ISRAEL
886–885 BC
1 Kings 16:12,13

PEKAH
KING OF ISRAEL
740–732 BC
2 Kings 15:27,28

MOSTLY DISOBEYED GOD

JEHOASH
KING OF ISRAEL
798–782 BC
2 Kings 13:11

OMRI
KING OF ISRAEL
880–874 BC
1 Kings 16:25,26

DON'T KNOW!

JEROBOAM I
KING OF ISRAEL
931–910 BC
1 Kings 13:33,34

ZECHARIAH
KING OF ISRAEL
753–752 BC
2 Kings 15:8,9

AHAZIAH
KING OF ISRAEL
853–852 BC
2 Kings 1:15,16

TIBNI
KING OF ISRAEL
885–880 BC
1 Kings 16:21,22

BAASHA
KING OF ISRAEL
909–886 BC
1 Kings 15:33,34

PEKANIAH
KING OF ISRAEL
742–740 BC
2 Kings 15:23,24

JEHOAHAZ
KING OF ISRAEL
814–798 BC
2 Kings 13:1,2

SHALLUM
KING OF ISRAEL
752 BC
2 Kings 15:13

TRIBAL RIVALS

FAITHFUL TO FAITHLESS THE PEOPLE. FAITHFUL, STILL FAITHFUL THEIR GOD.

THE EXILE IN BABYLON

AIMS

To help group members:

- **discover that, at the time of the exile, God faithfully kept his promises to his people – the situation wasn't hopeless**
- **handle times when they feel far away from God themselves.**

SCOPE

In spite of the prophets' warnings, God's people didn't worship and obey him wholeheartedly. Israel, the northern kingdom, was destroyed by the Assyrians. Then in 586 BC, after 18 months of siege, the Babylonians broke through Jerusalem's walls. They destroyed the city. Under King Nebuchadnezzar's orders, the survivors were taken to Babylon. Only the poorest workers were left in Judah to farm the land.

BIBLE BASE

2 Kings 25:8–21; Psalm 137; Isaiah 55:6–13

MATERIALS AND EQUIPMENT

For your own preparation and for other parts of the session, you'll need:

- your Leader Theme Card (page 7) and Bible
- overhead projector and screen (optional)
- name badges for the prophets Joel, Isaiah, Jeremiah, Zephaniah and Micah
- sheets of Avery labels L7160 (21 labels per A4 sheet) with the prophets' messages (page 45) photocopied onto them
- a notepad and pen
- a whistle
- an 'aristocratic' suit with all the trimmings (someone must have one!)
- thick felt-tip pens
- an enlarged version of the session **Symbol** and **Shout** (page 46) on an overhead projector acetate or paper
- the Theme Scoreboard

PREPARATION

DO 'YOUR OWN TIME' WITH GOD' (SEE BELOW). FAMILIARISE YOURSELF WITH THE SESSION OUTLINE. MAKE SURE YOU'RE CLEAR HOW THE GAME WORKS. NEAR YOUR USUAL MEETING ROOM FIND A SUITABLE AREA WITH HIDING PLACES WHERE YOU CAN PLAY THE GAME. GET TOGETHER ALL THE MATERIALS AND EQUIPMENT YOU NEED.

YOUR OWN TIME WITH GOD

Grasp the events of the fall of Jerusalem and the exile from 2 Kings 25:8–21 using your Leader Theme Card. Now put yourself in an exile's shoes as you read Psalm 137. Which three words or phrases would you use to sum up your feelings? Notice that this is not a song of hopelessness, but of defiant loyalty (verse 5).

If you feel cut off from God or battered and bruised by the tough things in your life, tell God about those feelings. God challenged his people to turn away from the wrong they had done because their struggles were a direct result of their disobedience. Yours may not be. But honest confession and remembering the certainty of God's forgiveness is something you may want to try.

> **READ**
> 2 KINGS 25:8–21;
> PSALM 137;
> ISAIAH 55:6–13

Sometimes you may not so much feel distant from God as estranged from the world. That shouldn't surprise you. After all, you belong in heaven, not here. Ask God to help you to live for him in that situation and pray about your impact on those around who don't know him. Pray for your group members in a similar way, especially any who might feel alienated from everyone and everything.

900 BC | 700 BC | 600 BC | 500 BC

BIBLE EVENTS

All dates approximate

722 BC Samaria falls to the Assyrians; Israel is destroyed.

605 BC Nebuchadnezzar II of Babylon defeats the Egyptians at Carchemish and brings Judah under Babylonian control.

586 BC Nebuchadnezzar II captures Jerusalem; the people are taken to Babylon.

OTHER WORLD EVENTS

776 BC The first Olympic Games are held in Greece.

753 BC According to tradition, Romulus and Remus found Rome.

626 BC The downfall of the Assyrian Empire begins when Babylon revolts.

609 BC The Assyrian Empire comes to an end.

581 BC The Greek philosopher Pythagoras is born.

580 BC Nebuchadnezzar II builds the Hanging Gardens of Babylon.

563 BC Siddhartha Gautama is born in India – he became the Buddha.

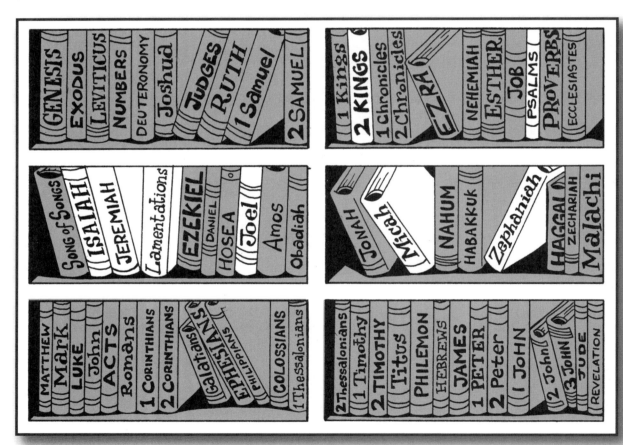

HANDY HINT

When playing runaround games like this one, always have plenty of adult supervisors to watch for safe play. Adults should not join in with such games because physical contact is probable and a hurtling adult might clash with a more fragile 13-year-old, causing injury.

Keep the aristocratic outfit hidden at the start. A leader should change into it before the end of the Scheme ready to appear as Isaiah.

Before the session begins, discreetly choose up to five group members who don't mind running and ask them to be the chasers in the **Scheme** game. No more than one third of the group should be chasers. They shouldn't tell anyone else that they have been chosen.

 10

SCENE-SETTER

Play a quick game of 'Alien'. Sit in a circle. An alien has landed on earth. It attacks people's faces. To demonstrate, spread the fingers of one hand over your face. Squeeze then let your face loose again in quick succession. The alien is now on your face – make horrible squelching noises! The person to your left must raise their right hand above their head and go 'wooo-wooo-wooo' as a warning siren; the person to your right must do the same with their left hand. After a few seconds, mime pulling the alien off your face and throwing it at someone else. The person with the alien and those either side do the same actions as before. Throw the alien round the circle until someone fails to do the actions or make the sounds in time. They're out. Keep going until there are only one, two or three people left – the winners.

Introduce the **Scheme** in this way:
In the northern kingdom of Israel and the southern kingdom of Judah, God's people and their kings were lying, cheating and worshipping other gods. You could hardly tell the difference between them and all the pagan tribes around them! But God loved them so much that he sent prophets to warn them. Hosea and Amos told the people of Israel that the Assyrians would wipe them out if they didn't get back to living God's way. The people of Israel ignored them and, sure enough, the Assyrians carted them off to Assyria as prisoners. They never came back. That was the end of Israel! But Judah escaped until…

 30

SCHEME

In this wide game the chasers represent the prophets Joel, Isaiah, Jeremiah, Zephaniah and Micah. (If there are fewer than five chasers, then each can represent more than one prophet.) They try to deliver their prophetic messages by sticking labels onto everyone else. The others run away and probably ignore what has been stuck on them. A mistake, as they discover too late!

Go outside to a playing area unless you have a big enough space indoors. Point out clearly the limits of the area – this is Judah. Tell everyone that they're the people of Judah. Divide the non-chasers into roughly equal teams. Note down who is in which team. Explain to the 'people of Judah' that chasers are going to try to stick labels on them. If caught, they can choose to take the label off and stick it on someone from another team, or to leave it alone. Be deliberately ambiguous about whether having labels is a good or bad thing. No labels must be destroyed or dropped. Also, there should be no physical contact except a label being pressed on. Disqualification follows any rough stuff! Don't say at this stage that the chasers represent prophets.

Explain that you'll blow a whistle to start the game and the 'people of Judah' will go to hide. One minute later another whistle blow will warn them that the chasers are coming. Ten minutes later the whistle will blow to end the game – no more labels can be fixed onto players, and everyone must make their way back to the start point.

As the 'people of Judah' run to hide, hand the chasers their 'prophet' name badges and a good supply of the message labels that go with them (see page 45).

At the end of the game, ask each team to count how many labels they have between them. The team with the smallest number wins according to the normal rules. Give them a cheer. Unfortunately, however, the normal rules don't apply.

Explain that the chasers were prophets. Get the 'prophets' to read out their name badges. The labels were warnings from God that the people of Judah should have welcomed. So the winning team should actually be the one that got the most labels and can recall the gist of as many of the five messages as possible – without looking. Get them to try it.

End the **Scheme** like this: *The people of Judah should have taken notice of God's warnings. They ignored them, and so the army of the Babylonians – the latest local superpower – swept through Judah, destroyed Jerusalem and carted off the survivors to Babylonia. We call the 70 years they spent there the 'exile'.*

Return to your usual meeting place and huddle uncomfortably in a corner behind some kind of barrier. Even better, go into 'exile' in a horrible, dingy place: smelly changing rooms or a cleaning cupboard – as long as it's safe. Read out 2 Kings 25:8–21.

Say something like this: *So where are the prophets now that we need them? Well, Ezekiel and Daniel are with us in exile and try to encourage us. They say that God won't let this be the end of us. There's new life just around the corner but only if we're sorry for all the wrong we've done. Isaiah the prophet had once looked ahead to these days and said...*

Immediately have your aristocratic Isaiah burst in and read out Isaiah 55:6–13.

SYMBOL AND SHOUT

Back in your usual meeting place, display the 'Exile' **Symbol** and **Shout** (page 46). Chant the **Shout** together until you have learnt it by heart. Leave the **Symbol** and **Shout** up for the rest of the session.

SCOREBOARD

Display the Theme Scoreboard. Sitting in their game teams, get everyone to discuss where any of the themes has occurred in today's session. Hand out pens to five confident writers. Invite each team to say where they spotted the themes. Ask the writers to note any correct suggestions on the appropriate part of the Scoreboard. Add your thoughts from 'Your own time with God'.

Be energetic about doing the 'Exile' **Shout** together.

SPACE

Send your group members as far away from each other as possible though still within the place where you meet. They'll need to be very self–disciplined about this. Invite them to:
- tell God how close to him or far away from him they feel
- make a move closer to him by asking him to be Lord of their lives, by saying sorry for the wrong in them or by planning to pray and read their Bible more often... or all of those!

You could give out these instructions on small cards or an overhead projector acetate. Clearly they can choose whether they want to do this activity or not – as long as they don't disturb anyone else.

Everyone should leave the session quietly after five minutes when they have finished both these prayer suggestions.

READ
2 KINGS 25:8–21
ISAIAH 55:6–13

PROPHET'S MESSAGE LABELS

'SOME DAY YOU WILL BEG THE LORD TO HELP YOU, BUT HE WILL TURN AWAY BECAUSE OF YOUR SINS.'
Micah 3:4

'SOME DAY YOU WILL BEG THE LORD TO HELP YOU, BUT HE WILL TURN AWAY BECAUSE OF YOUR SINS.'
Micah 3:4

'SOME DAY YOU WILL BEG THE LORD TO HELP YOU, BUT HE WILL TURN AWAY BECAUSE OF YOUR SINS.'
Micah 3:4

'SOME DAY YOU WILL BEG THE LORD TO HELP YOU, BUT HE WILL TURN AWAY BECAUSE OF YOUR SINS.'
Micah 3:4

'SOME DAY YOU WILL BEG THE LORD TO HELP YOU, BUT HE WILL TURN AWAY BECAUSE OF YOUR SINS.'
Micah 3:4

'SOME DAY YOU WILL BEG THE LORD TO HELP YOU, BUT HE WILL TURN AWAY BECAUSE OF YOUR SINS.'
Micah 3:4

'SOUND THE TRUMPET ON ZION, THE LORD'S SACRED HILL. WARN EVERYONE TO TREMBLE! THE JUDGEMENT DAY OF THE LORD IS COMING SOON.'
Joel 2:1

'SOUND THE TRUMPET ON ZION, THE LORD'S SACRED HILL. WARN EVERYONE TO TREMBLE! THE JUDGEMENT DAY OF THE LORD IS COMING SOON.'
Joel 2:1

'SOUND THE TRUMPET ON ZION, THE LORD'S SACRED HILL. WARN EVERYONE TO TREMBLE! THE JUDGEMENT DAY OF THE LORD IS COMING SOON.'
Joel 2:1

'SOUND THE TRUMPET ON ZION, THE LORD'S SACRED HILL. WARN EVERYONE TO TREMBLE! THE JUDGEMENT DAY OF THE LORD IS COMING SOON.'
Joel 2:1

'SOUND THE TRUMPET ON ZION, THE LORD'S SACRED HILL. WARN EVERYONE TO TREMBLE! THE JUDGEMENT DAY OF THE LORD IS COMING SOON.'
Joel 2:1

'SOUND THE TRUMPET ON ZION, THE LORD'S SACRED HILL. WARN EVERYONE TO TREMBLE! THE JUDGEMENT DAY OF THE LORD IS COMING SOON.'
Joel 2:1

'YOU ARE HEADED FOR TROUBLE! YOU SAY WRONG IS RIGHT, DARKNESS IS LIGHT, AND BITTER IS SWEET.'
Isaiah 5:20

'YOU ARE HEADED FOR TROUBLE! YOU SAY WRONG IS RIGHT, DARKNESS IS LIGHT, AND BITTER IS SWEET.'
Isaiah 5:20

'YOU ARE HEADED FOR TROUBLE! YOU SAY WRONG IS RIGHT, DARKNESS IS LIGHT, AND BITTER IS SWEET.'
Isaiah 5:20

'BUT JERUSALEM, THERE IS STILL TIME FOR YOU TO BE SAVED. WASH THE EVIL FROM YOUR HEARTS AND STOP MAKING SINFUL PLANS.'
Jeremiah 4:14

'BUT JERUSALEM, THERE IS STILL TIME FOR YOU TO BE SAVED. WASH THE EVIL FROM YOUR HEARTS AND STOP MAKING SINFUL PLANS.'
Jeremiah 4:14

'BUT JERUSALEM, THERE IS STILL TIME FOR YOU TO BE SAVED. WASH THE EVIL FROM YOUR HEARTS AND STOP MAKING SINFUL PLANS.'
Jeremiah 4:14

'TOO BAD FOR THAT DISGUSTING, CORRUPT, AND LAWLESS CITY! FOREVER REBELLIOUS AND REJECTING CORRECTION, JERUSALEM REFUSES TO TRUST OR OBEY THE LORD GOD.'
Zephaniah 3:1,2

'TOO BAD FOR THAT DISGUSTING, CORRUPT, AND LAWLESS CITY! FOREVER REBELLIOUS AND REJECTING CORRECTION, JERUSALEM REFUSES TO TRUST OR OBEY THE LORD GOD.'
Zephaniah 3:1,2

'TOO BAD FOR THAT DISGUSTING, CORRUPT, AND LAWLESS CITY! FOREVER REBELLIOUS AND REJECTING CORRECTION, JERUSALEM REFUSES TO TRUST OR OBEY THE LORD GOD.'
Zephaniah 3:1,2

EXILE

DON'T GIVE UP YOUR HOPE;
JUST DUMP WHAT'S WRONG.
TURN BACK TO GOD,
WHERE YOU BELONG.

THE RETURN FROM EXILE

AIMS

To help group members:
- **understand God's faithfulness and the peace that he brings**
- **pray in the light of what they have discovered about God**

SCOPE

God's people returned from exile in Babylon and, with Nehemiah's help, rebuilt the gates and walls of Jerusalem.

BIBLE BASE

Nehemiah 2,3; Psalm 122

MATERIALS AND EQUIPMENT

Arrange the following for each team of players:
- three Bibles
- a Game Card (page 51) enlarged to A4
- a Game Map of Jerusalem (page 51) enlarged to A3
- a thick felt-tip pen

For your own preparation and for other parts of the session, you'll need:
- your copy of the Leader Theme Card (page 7) and Bible
- a Nehemiah costume (eg waiter's gear with a builder's hard hat)
- an overhead projector and screen (optional)
- coloured paper for drawing
- sticky tape or Blu-tack
- thick felt-tip pens
- the Theme Scoreboard
- an enlarged version of the session **Symbol** and **Shout** (page 52) on overhead projector acetate or paper

PREPARATION

DO 'YOUR OWN TIME WITH GOD' (SEE BELOW). FAMILIARISE YOURSELF WITH THE SESSION OUTLINE. GET TOGETHER ALL THE MATERIALS AND EQUIPMENT YOU'LL NEED. MAKE SURE THAT ALL THE ITEMS MENTIONED ON THE GAME CARD (PAGE 51) CAN BE FOUND SOMEWHERE NEAR WHERE YOU RUN YOUR SESSION.

YOUR OWN TIME WITH GOD

Read the whole book of Nehemiah, if you can (it will probably take about 15 minutes!), but at least chapters 2 and 3. Note on your Leader Theme Card any hints of the five themes. Nehemiah's main concern about Jerusalem was that God had chosen it to represent his name. To outsiders, a ruin of a city would suggest a ruin of a God. Also, a city without walls would make the people vulnerable, belying one possible meaning of the city's name. 'Jeruslem' (with echoes of the Hebrew word for 'peace' or 'wholeness' – 'shalom') suggested a 'city of peace' and security. The Jews had to survive for God's long-term plan to work out.

Read Psalm 122, probably a song that pilgrims sang on their way up to Jerusalem for one of the four major annual festivals. Imagine entering Jerusalem among an excited crowd of pilgrims. Notice the architecture of the temple, the gates and the towers ('citadels'). This is the city of God. Ask yourself:
- So what does the psalm tell me about God?
- So what does it help me express to God?

Thank God for the peace and security you have in him through Christ, and pray for peace, security and unity in your church. Pray too that your group will understand God's faithfulness and that they will experience his peace and security.

READ
NEHEMIAH 2,3,
PSALM 122

600 BC → **550 BC** → **500 BC** → **450 BC**

BIBLE EVENTS

All dates approximate

586 BC — The fall of Jerusalem – the city and temple are destroyed by the Babylonians; the Jews are taken into exile.

539 BC — Persian King Cyrus takes over Babylonia and allows the Jews home.

536 BC — The rebuilding of the temple begins.

520–515 BC — Work continues until the temple is finished.

445 BC — Nehemiah is appointed governor of Judah.

440(?) BC — Nehemiah returns to Jerusalem and rebuilds the walls.

428(?) BC — Ezra, a scholar and Jewish priest, returns to Jerusalem with more exiles and re-establishes religious practices.

OTHER WORLD EVENTS

600 BC — Early cities develop in the Ganges Valley, India.

581 BC — The Greek philosopher Pythagoras is born.

580 BC — Nebuchadnezzar builds the Hanging Gardens of Babylon.

563 BC — Siddhartha Gautama (later to become the Buddha) is born in India.

551 BC — K'ung Fu-tzu (Confucius) is born in China.

510 BC — In Rome the people rebel against Tarquinius Superbus, the last king of Rome.

500 BC — Around this time is the high point of Greek philosophy.

485 BC — The Persian King Darius dies; Xerxes takes over, marking the beginning of the decline of the great Persian Empire.

450 BC — The Twelve Tables of Roman Laws are created – wooden tablets on which the laws of Rome are written.

429 BC — In Athens the Acropolis is finished.

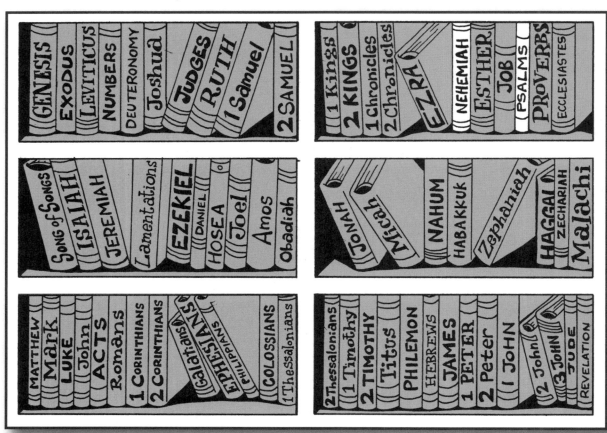

HANDY HINT

With fairly boisterous activities like this, it is best to have one leader with each small team of group members. Leaders should join in with the team allowing themselves to be led. Their role is to encourage everyone to join in, and to see that their team plays fairly and does not behave dangerously.

GATES AND WALLS

Stay dressed as Nehemiah throughout this session. How about a waiter's outfit with one or two items of builder's gear such as a hard hat or covering of brick dust? You'll feel pretty daft, but everyone else will love it!

 15

SCENE-SETTER

Get everyone to put the chairs round the edge of the room and to sit on the floor in teams of no more than four. If you have four or fewer group members you could stay as one team.

Tell them you're all Jews who have returned from exile in Babylonia. Ask them what they remember about Session 6 ('Exile'). You're now back home in Jerusalem but the city is in ruins.

Introduce yourself as Nehemiah – 'the Governor'. Explain that you're a Jew who used to taste the wine of the Persian king in Babylonia to check that it wasn't poisoned. But you were more than happy to give up that amazingly important job in order to become governor of the tiny land of Judah, which included Jerusalem.

Give each team a map of Jerusalem and a felt pen. Get them to follow Nehemiah's route as you read aloud (and perhaps even act out) Nehemiah 2:11–20. Then one member of each team, helped by the others, should draw the route on the map.

Tell your group that you plan to rebuild all the walls and gates of Jerusalem. Explain why. (See 'Your own time with God' on page 47.) Get everyone to build the city wall by positioning chairs so the layout is the same as on the map. If you have enough space, show each gate by leaving a gap big enough to run through. If not, just make two gateways.

Now divide up all the gate names among the teams. Get them to design gate labels using paper and felt pens. They should stick each one by the right gateway or, if you have less space, to a chair at the right point in the 'wall'.

  5

SYMBOL AND SHOUT

Display the 'Gates and walls' **Symbol** and **Shout** (page 52). Have fun learning it by heart all together, then make sure it keeps on appearing at different points in the session, not necessarily on show all the time.

 25

SCHEME

Tell each team to find a 'home' inside the 'city' and sit down in it together. Appoint a team leader for each team.

Give each team leader a 'Gates and walls' Game Card (page 51). The team should read and take in the rules at the top of the Game Card. Allow the team leader **three minutes only** to allocate challenges fairly. Not all challenges will involve everyone on the team.

Team members must run through the appropriate gateway on the return stretch of each challenge. If you do not have all the gateways, they must simply touch the appropriate gate label before returning 'home'.

When the members of a team put up their hands you should check they have completed the challenge and set them off on their next one. The team leader should tick off each challenge on the Game Card. Use a Game Card yourself as a master score-sheet to help you keep track of how the teams are doing.

Before they begin, explain: *When you hear the warning 'Attack! Attack! Attack!', everyone must leave what they're doing and get back to their 'home' inside the city walls within thirty seconds. At the end of the time any team that has all players at 'home' will gain one bonus point. Then wait at 'home' for another instruction!*

GATES AND WALLS

READ
NEHEMIAH 2,3;
PSALM 122

Shout 'Attack! Attack! Attack!' three times during the game. When all the players are 'home' instruct them to do the following:

- **The first time, say:**
  Open your three Bibles at the 'Safety verses' shown on your Game Card. Leave them open at the right places and get on with the game.
- **The second time, say:**
  Look at the 'Safety verses'. In each Bible passage find one thing it says about God – something he says, does or is. As soon as everyone in the team can remember the three things by heart, get on with the game.
- **The third time, say:**
  Write on the back of your Game Map the three things you said about God last time. Then get on with the game.

If you want this **Scheme** to be competitive, the first team to complete all its challenges wins. If not, let everyone race against the clock, allowing them a generous amount of time to finish everything.

SCOREBOARD

Stay in the same teams to think about the five themes. Read out the questions below one at a time, giving the teams only about one minute to discuss each. Remind them that they may not be able to find some of the themes – that's OK. From this Bible event:

- Is God creating anything good? If so, what?
- Is he promising anything? If so, what?
- Is he showing anything about himself? If so, what and how?
- Is he judging anyone? If so, who and why?
- Is he saving anyone? If so, who and how?

Add the question: Is God doing anything else?

Collate feedback from the teams, carefully questioning any of their answers that don't seem to tie in with what the Bible says. As you do so, feed in any of your own insights from reading the rest of Nehemiah and Psalm 122. As each team has a turn, get the others to delete any facts on their lists which have already been mentioned.

Invite each team to graffiti the comments remaining on their lists onto the Theme Scoreboard.

SPACE

Once again, huddle in teams in the security of the 'city walls'. Encourage the group members, silently or out loud, to praise God for something written on the Theme Scoreboard.

Now (hopefully!) quietly and prayerfully, ask them to pray about their own lives:

- Is God making something good and new happen in you or for you?
- Have you been reminded of any of God's promises recently?
- What has he recently shown you about himself?
- Is he showing you that there is something wrong in your life?
- Is he saving or protecting you from something that will harm you?

Finish by yelling the 'Gates and walls' **Shout** together.

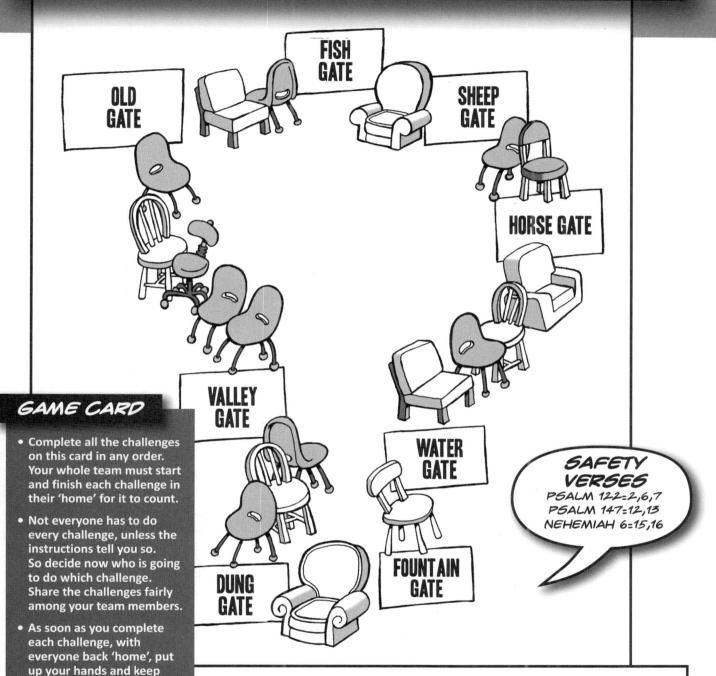

SAFETY VERSES
PSALM 12:2=2,6,7
PSALM 147=12,13
NEHEMIAH 6:15,16

GAME CARD

- Complete all the challenges on this card in any order. Your whole team must start and finish each challenge in their 'home' for it to count.

- Not everyone has to do every challenge, unless the instructions tell you so. So decide now who is going to do which challenge. Share the challenges fairly among your team members.

- As soon as you complete each challenge, with everyone back 'home', put up your hands and keep them there until your team has been noticed. Then tick the challenge you've completed and start another one.

- Now before you begin, wait for instructions about what to do when you hear the warning 'Attack! Attack! Attack!'

■ **Old Gate**
Add up the ages of all your team members. One of you must go through the Old Gate and queue to tell the Governor your answer.

■ **Valley Gate**
Bring seven leaves in through the Valley Gate and when you're all sitting down, wave them above your heads.

■ **Water Gate**
Bring three cups of water in through the Water Gate.

■ **Sheep Gate**
Bring two woollen jumpers in through the Sheep Gate.

■ **Horse Gate**
Two team members must gallop on all fours out of the Horse Gate, right around the city and back in through the Horse Gate.

■ **Fountain Gate**
Bring back through the Fountain Gate three items to do with drinking – not the three cups of water from the Water Gate!

■ **Dung Gate**
Bring six sheets of toilet paper in through the Dung Gate.

■ **Fish Gate**
Make one paper fish and bring it in through the Fish Gate back to your team.

GATES AND WALLS

GOD NEVER GIVES UP.
SO WHAT HAVE WE GOT?
NOT A CITY IN PIECES
BUT GOD'S CITY AT PEACE.

JESUS AND THE HOLY SPIRIT

AIMS

To help group members:
- understand that Jesus is right at the centre of absolutely everything, as the focus of God's big plan
- see how Jesus turns the rules of earthly kingdoms upside down
- have the opportunity to respond personally to Jesus.

SCOPE

Jesus' life, death, resurrection and ascension to heaven, and the coming of the Holy Spirit

BIBLE BASE

Matthew 5:1–12; Luke 4:16–21; John 3:16–18; Colossians 1:15–23

MATERIALS AND EQUIPMENT

For each pair of group members you'll need:
- a set of Game Cards (page 57), enlarged to A3, cut up and shuffled

For your own preparation and for other parts of the session, you'll need:
- your copy of the Leader Theme Card (page 7) and Bible
- an overhead projector and screen (optional)
- pens
- thick felt-tip pens
- tablecloths
- white pieces of card for everyone to make a place name for themselves
- plastic cups
- white paper plates
- red grape juice
- one small bread roll per person
- a wooden cross made of two rough pieces of wood nailed together
- a light hammer
- small nails
- strips of brightly coloured paper cut from A4
- the Theme Scoreboard
- an enlarged version of 'Jesus' (page 58) on overhead projector acetate or paper
- background music on tape or CD
- tape or CD player
- an enlarged version of the session **Symbol** and **Shout** (page 59) on overhead projector acetate or paper

PREPARATION

DO 'YOUR OWN TIME WITH GOD' (SEE BELOW), THEN CHECK OUT THE SESSION OUTLINE. THERE IS DELIBERATELY LESS GAME TIME, AND MORE THINKING AND RESPONSE TIME THIS SESSION – IT'S QUIETER, BUT HOPEFULLY NO LESS STIMULATING. GET TOGETHER ALL THE MATERIALS AND EQUIPMENT YOU NEED.

YOUR OWN TIME WITH GOD

If you have time, write a letter to God thanking him for who Jesus is and what he has done. Ask God to show you anything you may have missed about Jesus as you read Colossians 1:15–23. What do these verses say about the beginning of everything? About what Jesus achieved through his death on the cross? About what he's doing right now? About what he will do in the future? As you hear echoes of our five themes, jot them down on your Leader Theme Card.

Now explore Matthew 5:1–12, Luke 4:16–21 and John 3:16–18, noticing how Jesus' ways of building God's heavenly kingdom were so different from the way in which earthly kingdoms had been built throughout history. Which values did Jesus turn upside down?

Pray for your group members as they have the opportunity in this session to respond to who Jesus is and to what he has done.

> **READ**
> MATTHEW 5:1–12;
> LUKE 4:16–21;
> JOHN 3:16–18;
> COLOSSIANS
> 1:15–23

50 BC → AD 50

BIBLE EVENTS

Most dates approximate

4 BC — Jesus is born.

AD 27 — Jesus is baptised by John – the start of Jesus' public ministry.

AD 30 — Jesus is arrested and killed at Passover time. He is raised from the dead and ascends into heaven. The Holy Spirit comes to Jesus' followers at Pentecost.

AD 32 — Paul is converted.

AD 34 — Paul pays his first visit to Jerusalem.

OTHER WORLD EVENTS

44 BC — Julius Caesar is assassinated; Mark Anthony seizes power.

42 BC — Caesar is declared a god.

40 BC — Herod the Great is king of Judea (to 4 BC).

27 BC — Octavian has supreme power in Rome and takes the title 'Augustus'.

19 BC — Herod the Great begins rebuilding the temple in Jerusalem.

AD 5 — Rome acknowledges Cymbeline as King of Britain.

AD 14 — Tiberius succeeds Augustus as emperor of Rome.

AD 26 — Pontius Pilate is treasury officer (procurator) for the Romans in Judea.

AD 33 — Taoism flourishes under Chang Tao-ling in China (to AD 156).

AD 37 — Tiberius dies; Gaius 'Caligula' takes over as emperor of Rome.

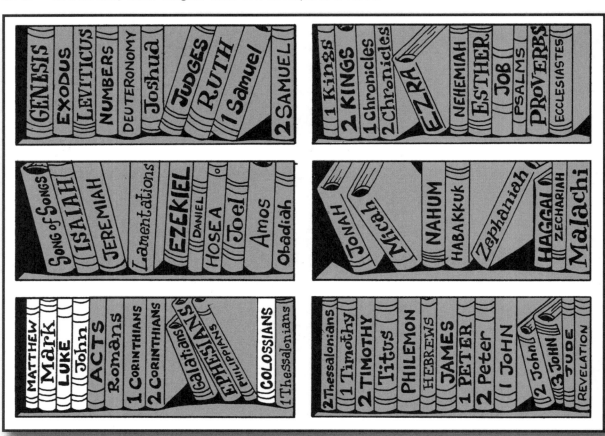

HANDY HINT

In this session it's important to establish a calm, reflective atmosphere in the group. If this seems about as likely as next door's budgie learning to juggle three car tyres, try:

- talking to any potentially restless group members before the session, asking for their special cooperation
- playing restful background music as the group arrives
- gathering them straight into an activity rather than allowing them time to run around or start mischief
- having as many adult leaders working closely with as few group members as possible all through the session

SCENE-SETTER

Play some gentle background music. Involve your group members in setting up a banquet for themselves: getting out tables and chairs (or allocating floor space), putting out tablecloths, making place settings laid with a plate and cup, and creating personalised place names for everyone. If you want to go crazy with any other decorations or, for instance, by putting flowers on the table, feel free! Get everyone to choose their own place according to the pairs or threes they wish to stay in for the rest of the session. Explain that you'll be having a 'kind of meal'.

Get everyone seated in their places, in their pairs or threes, and introduce the **Scheme** in this way:
We've met quite a few kings already in the Bible – many of them bloodthirsty, power-mad and out for success. But when God's chosen king, the Messiah, arrived things were very different. He was Jesus. We read about him in the Bible books of Matthew, Mark, Luke and John. Jesus wasn't into building kingdoms by wars, armies, power and success, but by teaching God's upside-down rules for living, and by dying for everyone. This must have seemed really weird! Jesus didn't actually call himself 'Messiah', though he accepted it when other people called him 'Messiah'. More often he called himself the 'Son of Man'. Yes, he was the great king from God, doing what God wanted in God's way, but he was also human and would suffer.

SCHEME

This game involves some of the world's old rules for living and some of Jesus' new rules. It can either be a race against the clock or against the other teams if you're happy with it being competitive.

Give a set of Game Cards (page 57) to each pair or three. One person should spread out the cards face down in the middle of all the players. The first player turns over two cards to see if they are opposites – the old rule which shows how most people live and Jesus' upside-down rule. If they aren't opposites, he or she has to turn them face down again. The second person has a turn, and so on. As soon as a pair of cards is matched, it is put to one side. Clearly the way to win is to memorize where each card is as it is turned over. It does get progressively easier to match the pairs – honestly! The first team to pair all their cards correctly wins. You should check that they have the right pairings before you declare them the winners. If they have made a mistake, get them to re–sort their cards until they think they have the right solution.

The cards are based on Jesus' teaching in Matthew 5:1–12. See page 57 for the correct pairings.

End the **Scheme** something like this: *Through his life and his words it's as if Jesus was saying, 'Forget all the ideas you've had about fighting and kingdoms. I'm not that kind of king and I don't want you to live like that. The real kingdom where God rules is in you. If you obey him and believe in me, you're already in his kingdom as one of his people. You will be saved from the worst that can happen to you... no, not from the Romans, but from being separated from God for ever. I came to save you from that kind of death.' But Jesus the King would save people in a strange kind of way.*

Bring on the wooden cross.

KINGDOM RULES

When Jesus and his disciples met for their last evening meal together, Jesus asked them to remember him – and what he was going to do with his body and blood – every time they ate bread and drank wine.

Give a bread roll to each person. For hygiene reasons, make sure you don't touch it with your bare hand. Pour out the grape juice for everyone.
Encourage everyone to eat and drink as you play some gentle background music and a leader reads out John 3:16–18.

SYMBOL AND SHOUT

Display the 'Kingdom rules' **Symbol** and **Shout** (page 59). Say it all together as a whisper then leave it up for the rest of the session.

SCOREBOARD

Show the sheet 'Jesus' (page 58), and explain what it all means. In their pairs or threes, get everyone to put each of the five statements into their own words. Ask one pair or three only to say what they have decided, then get the others to try to improve on it. Finally write up the best version yourself on the Scoreboard.

SPACE

Give each person a pen and a slip of brightly coloured paper. Invite them to write down a personal response to what Jesus did on the cross. What do they want to say to him about it? They should write honestly even if they feel apathetic or negative about it. No one should look at anyone else's slip as it is being written. If they don't want to say anything at all, they should write the word 'Nothing' on their slip, but still do the activity.

Get everyone to fold their slip in half. As some quiet music plays in the background, they should come forward one at a time to the cross, pick up the hammer and a small nail, and pin their message to the cross. At the same time, they can speak their words to Jesus silently in prayer, if they want to. They return to their place and the next person goes forward. If your group is large, have two hammers and get your group members to come up in pairs.

Finish the session in this way: *Jesus' followers were all gathered together. The awful thing that had happened was staring them in the face.*

They were all gathered together when the fantastic news broke that Jesus was alive again.

They were all gathered together some weeks later too, but this time it was Pentecost, a time of wild rejoicing and thanksgiving for God's gift at harvest. Crowds of Jews massed in Jerusalem from all over the Eastern Mediterranean lands to celebrate Pentecost. Jesus had gone back into heaven, but he'd promised to send someone to help his followers – the Holy Spirit. And sure enough, the Holy Spirit came, like fire, like wind. Now the Holy Spirit would help them to do what God wanted, in God's way, with God's energy. Jesus' influence wouldn't be limited to one little country where Jesus lived and died. By the Holy Spirit, he would be with all his people everywhere, as we shall see next time.

TRULY HAPPY ARE THOSE WHO REALISE THEY'RE NOT PERFECT AND THEY NEED GOD.

TRULY HAPPY ARE THOSE WHO THINK THEY'RE OK JUST AS THEY ARE AND DON'T NEED GOD OR ANYONE ELSE.

TRULY HAPPY ARE THOSE WHO ARE SAD BECAUSE THEY SEE WRONG IN THEMSELVES AND IN THE WORLD.

TRULY HAPPY ARE THOSE WHO ALWAYS LOOK ON THE BRIGHT SIDE LIFE AND DON'T BOTHER ABOUT THE WRONG IN THEMSELVES AND IN THE WORLD.

TRULY HAPPY ARE THOSE WHO REALISE JUST WHO AND WHAT THEY ARE, AND WHO PUT OTHERS FIRST.

TRULY HAPPY ARE THOSE WHO THINK THEY'RE THE BEST, AND DON'T CARE ABOUT ANYONE ELSE.

TRULY HAPPY ARE THOSE WHO FORGIVE OTHER PEOPLE AND GIVE GENEROUSLY. GOD WILL FORGIVE THEM AND BE GENEROUS TO THEM, TOO.

TRULY HAPPY ARE THOSE WHO GET THEIR OWN BACK ON OTHER PEOPLE.

TRULY HAPPY ARE THOSE WHO LIVE HONEST, SINCERE LIVES THAT BRING HONOUR TO GOD.

TRULY HAPPY ARE THOSE WHO WANT THE BEST IN LIFE FOR THEMSELVES AND DON'T CARE HOW THEY GET IT.

TRULY HAPPY ARE THOSE WHO HELP MAKE PEACE BETWEEN PEOPLE, EVEN IF IT COSTS THEM DEARLY.

TRULY HAPPY ARE THOSE WHO STIR UP TROUBLE BETWEEN PEOPLE, BUT STAY OUT OF IT THEMSELVES.

EVEN IF LIFE GETS REALLY TOUGH FOR CHRISTIANS, THEY KNOW THEY'RE OBEYING GOD AND WILL BE WITH HIM ONE DAY.

IF LIFE IS NICE AND EASY, WE KNOW WE'RE OK.

TRULY HAPPY ARE YOU WHEN PEOPLE GIVE YOU A TOUGH TIME FOR BELIEVING IN GOD. YOU CAN BE SURE OF A FANTASTIC WELCOME IN HEAVEN.

TRULY HAPPY ARE YOU WHEN YOU'RE REALLY POPULAR WITH EVERYONE.

JESUS

THE ONE

WHO FULFILS THE **PROMISE** GOD MADE TO SEND THE BEST KING EVER

WHO **SHOWS** PEOPLE EXACTLY WHAT GOD IS LIKE

WHO **SAVES** PEOPLE FROM THE WORST THAT COULD POSSIBLY HAPPEN TO THEM – DEATH FOREVER

WHOSE LIFE, DEATH AND RESURRECTION MEAN THAT PEOPLE CAN CHOOSE EITHER TO BELIEVE AND TRUST IN HIM, BE **JUDGED** AND FOUND INNOCENT BY GOD, OR TO REJECT HIM, BE **JUDGED** AND FOUND GUILTY BY GOD, AND BE SEPARATED FROM HIM FOR EVER

WHO **CREATES** NEW LIFE IN THOSE WHO BELIEVE AND TRUST IN HIM.

KINGDOM RULES

JESUS WAS GOD'S CHOSEN ONE,
HIS SON, TO GET GOD'S BEST JOB DONE.

EARLY CHURCHES

READ
ACTS 13,14

THE SPREAD OF GOD'S KINGDOM

AIMS
To help group members:
- explore the nature of the gospel and watch for God at work in this period of history
- recognise God at work in their own lives, or invite him to be

SCOPE
Paul's first missionary journey through Cyprus and Asia Minor

BIBLE BASE
Acts 13,14

MATERIALS AND EQUIPMENT
Arrange the following for each team of players:
- a Bible
- a reel of sticky tape
- a broadsheet newspaper
- a pen
- a photocopied Game Map and Game Card (page 63) enlarged to A4 or A3

For your own preparation and for other parts of the session, you'll need:
- your copy of the Leader Theme Card (page 7) and Bible
- four shatterproof bowls
- a box of Rice Krispies
- an overhead projector and screen (optional)
- a tent costume (yes, grab a small tent and get someone to wear it!)
- sticky tape or Blu-tack
- place names written large – 'Antioch in Syria', 'Paphos', 'Perga', 'Antioch in Pisidia', 'Iconium', 'Lystra', 'Derbe'
- seven sheets of coloured stickers – one sheet for each town with the town name written on each sticker
- a photocopied set of clues and Game Score Sheet (page 64)
- seven envelopes, each having one of the town names written on the outside
- thick felt-tip pens
- the Theme Scoreboard
- small candles with protective card shields – one for each person
- matches
- fire safety equipment
- an enlarged version of the session **Symbol** and **Shout** (page 65) on overhead projector acetate or paper

PREPARATION

DO 'YOUR OWN TIME WITH GOD' (SEE BELOW). PUT THE SHEETS OF PLACE-NAME STICKERS AND THE CLUES IN THE APPROPRIATE TOWN ENVELOPES. USE THE MAP ON PAGE 63 TO HELP YOU STICK UP THE TOWN NAMES AROUND YOUR ROOM IN ROUGHLY THE RIGHT GEOGRAPHICAL POSITION RELATIVE TO EACH OTHER. STICK EACH TOWN'S ENVELOPE NEAR THE TOWN NAME. CUT CIRCLES OF CARD THROUGH WHICH TO PUSH THE CANDLES. THESE WILL PROTECT HANDS FROM MELTING WAX.

YOUR OWN TIME WITH GOD
Pray for God's help to grasp for yourself the shape and significance of Paul's first missionary journey. Read Acts 13,14 pausing to note down on your Leader Theme Card any echoes of the five themes that you 'hear' as you go through. Even better, read Acts all the way through in one or two sittings.

Luke doesn't focus much on individuals' lives (though there are some mentioned) nor on the way the church was structured (though there is a little of that), but on the thrilling fact that the gospel spread rapidly. God was at work. The Holy Spirit was moving in people's lives. Whole communities were being changed because of God's word. There's a breath-taking relentlessness about it all – this is what God wanted to happen so this is what happened, in spite of all the difficulties and setbacks. Thank him that the good news of Jesus cannot be stopped. Pray that your group will be thrilled at the power of the gospel to bring people new life in Christ.

AD 25 > AD 50 > AD 75 > AD 100

BIBLE EVENTS

All dates approximate

AD 27	Jesus is baptised by John the Baptist.
AD 30	Jesus is crucified.
AD 32	Saul is converted to Christianity and becomes Paul.
AD 34	Paul visits Jerusalem.
AD 45	Paul begins his missionary journeys.
AD 45 or 46	Paul's first journey takes place.
AD 48–51	Paul's second journey takes place.
AD 53	Paul's third journey takes place.
AD 60	Paul is on trial before the Roman procurator, Festus.
AD 65	Mark's Gospel is possibly written at about this time.
AD 67	Peter and Paul are martyred in Rome.

OTHER WORLD EVENTS

AD 37	Roman Emperor Tiberius dies; Gaius 'Caligula' takes over.
AD 41	Caligula is assassinated; Claudius becomes emperor.
AD 43	Under Aulus Plautius the Romans invade Britain.
AD 54	Claudius is murdered; Nero becomes emperor.
AD 58	Emperor Ming-ti introduces Buddhism to China.
AD 61	Boadicea of the Iceni leads a revolt in Britain.
AD 64	Fire destroys Rome; Christians are blamed.
AD 68	There is rebellion in Rome; Nero commits suicide.

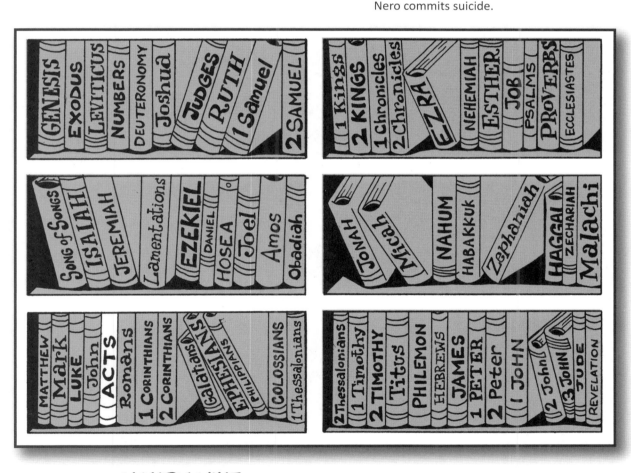

HANDY HINT

In action-packed sessions like this one, with group members having some autonomy, you rely heavily on their sense of commitment to the group. If that commitment is missing they may try to wreck the activity for everyone else. Group members can develop greater 'ownership' of the games if you encourage a few of them to help you plan and prepare them. In particular, involve those young people who you think are most likely to try to spoil things for others.

Get a leader to wear a tent throughout the session.

SCENE-SETTER

Play 'Krispie Feet'. It's a relay race in which players use their bare feet to transfer Rice Krispies from a bowl at one end of the room to a bowl at the other. Do it against the clock. It'll help everyone start thinking about passing on the good news of Jesus… naturally!

Introduce the **Scheme** in this way: *The good news about Jesus spread in some pretty strange ways! Saul was a Pharisee, a strict Jewish leader who tried to keep every detail of God's laws. He hated Jesus' followers and hunted them down. As he was travelling to Damascus to blitz some believers, Jesus spoke to him - and Saul ended up wanting to tell everyone about Jesus! His name was changed to Paul. From then on, instead of thrashing people for following Jesus, he suffered horrible things himself as he travelled round the Mediterranean region, helping people to get to know God.*

SYMBOL AND SHOUT

Display the 'Early churches' **Symbol** and Shout (page 65). Groove through the **Shout** as a rap and teach it to everyone else. Keep the **Symbol** and **Shout** visible right through the session.

SCHEME

Play in teams of three or more, ideally with an adult in each team. If you only have one team, race against the clock. Get each team to make a 'tent' with newspaper and sticky tape. It should be big enough for at least one person to get inside. They should fold their tent neatly ready to travel.

Explain that the teams will follow Paul's first journey round part of the Mediterranean. Like Paul, they will start at Antioch in Syria. They must follow the instructions on the Game Card. Go through these now. At the end of the journey, every team member will have to know what happened at each place in order, so they will have to teach each other.

Allow about 20 minutes for the journey. If there's more than one team, stagger the start. If possible, take waiting teams away from your room. Settle them down to look for the Scoreboard themes in the gospel message that Paul took round with him. Some of it is in Acts 13:16–33.

As each team finishes, check their time, Game Map and sticker order, and see if they know what happened at each place. Add ten penalty seconds for each mistake. The Game Score Sheet (page 64) should help.

SCOREBOARD

Collate theme feedback from the teams, carefully questioning any answers which don't tie up with what the Bible says. Add your own insights from reading Acts 13,14. Ask each team to graffiti their comments on the Theme Scoreboard.

SPACE

Be very careful during this activity. Give out candles. All huddle around the Theme Scoreboard, staying in teams. Hand each team leader a lighted candle. He or she should light the candle of one team member from it. Pass the light on from person to person until every candle is lit. Now ask them to pray quietly and thoughtfully:

- Who was the first person to pass on to you the light of the good news of Jesus?
- Is God making something bright and good happen in you just now?
- Has he recently shone a light on who he is for you?
- Is he showing up something that's wrong in your lives?
- Is he saving or protecting you from something that will harm you?

Finish by doing the 'Early churches' **Shout** together.

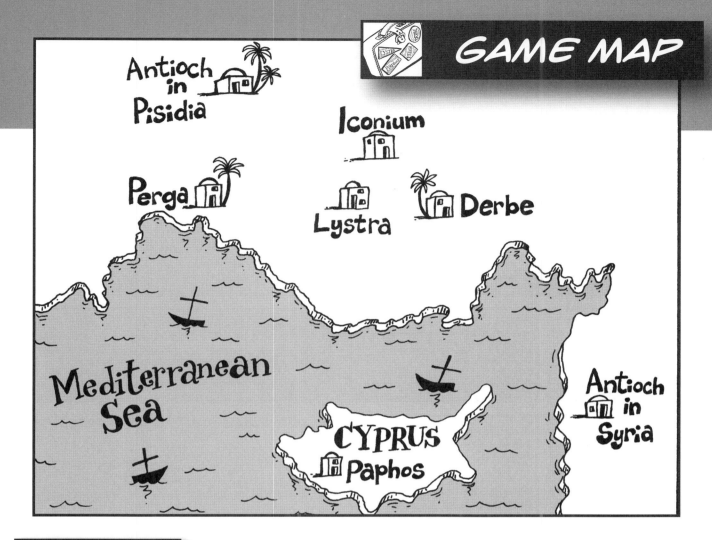

Antioch in Pisidia

Iconium

Perga

Lystra

Derbe

Mediterranean Sea

Antioch in Syria

CYPRUS
Paphos

GAME CARD

You will be following Paul's first journey round part of the Mediterranean. All teams will start at Antioch in Syria, where Paul started.

At each place on your journey, you must:
• plot your route on your map
• put up your tent with at least one person inside and everyone else holding it up
• collect a name sticker and stick it on this card to show the order in which you visit places
• collect a Clue Card and read all of it out loud to the team. Learn the FACT on the card and where it happened, and solve the CLUE for the next place to visit.

At the end of the journey your whole team will need to know what happened at each place in order. You'll have to teach each other as you go round.

If you're waiting to start, try to find what the Bible says about our five themes from some of what Paul taught on his first journey. Use the theme sheets and Acts 13:16–33.

When you get back to Antioch in Syria and put up your tent, you have finished. A leader will check your time, your Game Map and the order of your stickers. Remember, you'll need to know the story of what happened at every place on the journey. There will be ten penalty seconds for every mistake.

CLUES

1

AT= YOU'RE AT **ANTIOCH IN SYRIA**, READY TO START YOUR FIRST MISSIONARY JOURNEY.

CLUE= ACTS 13=6

REPLACE THIS CLUE IN THE ENVELOPE BEFORE YOU MOVE ON

2

AT= YOU'RE AT PAPHOS ON THE ISLAND OF CYPRUS.

FACT= THE MAGICIAN ELYMAS OPPOSES PAUL AND BARNABAS.

CLUE= ACTS 13=13

REPLACE THIS CLUE IN THE ENVELOPE BEFORE YOU MOVE ON

3

AT= YOU'RE AT **PERGA**.

FACT= PAUL AND BARNABAS' HELPER JOHN MARK LEAVES THEM AND GOES BACK TO JERUSALEM. ASK YOUR TEAM IF ANYONE WANTS TO DROP OUT, BUT ONLY ONE IS ALLOWED TO GO.

CLUE= ACTS 13=14

REPLACE THIS CLUE IN THE ENVELOPE BEFORE YOU MOVE ON

4

AT= YOU'RE AT ANTIOCH IN PISIDIA.

FACT= PAUL PREACHES TO THE JEWS AND NON-JEWS (GENTILES). THE JEWS ARE JEALOUS AND STIR UP TROUBLE.

CLUE= ACTS 14=1

REPLACE THIS CLUE IN THE ENVELOPE BEFORE YOU MOVE ON

5

AT= YOU'RE AT ICONIUM.

FACT= PAUL AND BARNABAS STAY A LONG TIME. MANY JEWS AND GENTILES BECOME BELIEVERS BUT SOME GENTILES PLOT TO STONE PAUL AND BARNABAS.

CLUE= ACTS 14=8

REPLACE THIS CLUE IN THE ENVELOPE BEFORE YOU MOVE ON

6

AT= YOU'RE AT LYSTRA.

FACT= PAUL HEALS A LAME MAN, AND PAUL AND BARNABAS ARE CHEERED AS GODS. BUT THEIR ENEMIES NEARLY KILL THEM.

CLUE= ACTS 14=21

REPLACE THIS CLUE IN THE ENVELOPE BEFORE YOU MOVE ON

7

AT= YOU'RE AT DERBE.

FACT= MANY MORE BECOME GOD'S PEOPLE.

CLUE= REVISIT ALL THE PLACES MENTIONED IN REVERSE ORDER, MISSING OUT PAPHOS, BUT ONLY BUILD A TENT AND GET A STICKER.

REPLACE THIS CLUE IN THE ENVELOPE BEFORE YOU MOVE ON

PLACE NAMES IN THE RIGHT ORDER

1. Antioch in Syria
2. Paphos
3. Perga
4. Antioch in Pisidia
5. Iconium
6. Lystra
7. Derbe
8. Lystra
9. Iconium
10. Antioch in Pisidia
11. Perga
12. Antioch in Syria

SCORE SHEET

	TEAM	TEAM	TEAM	TEAM
TIME				
PENALTY SECONDS (10 PER ERROR) FOR...				
STICKERS				
MAP				
KNOWLEDGE				

EARLY CHURCHES

THE TRUTH STILL SPREADS:
'BE ALIVE, NOT DEAD.
DON'T BE ODD,
BELONG TO GOD.
USE YOUR HEAD!'

JESUS' RETURN, REVELATION AND THE NEW CREATION

AIMS

To help group members:

- **grasp the fact that Jesus will return one day**
- **know that God's covenant with his people will be realised in heaven in the best possible way**
- **be bold about living for Christ even when life is tough, or be challenged to start living for him**

SCOPE

Jesus was raised from death, then ascended to heaven where he now lives with the Father. One day he will return as King – everyone will see him. He will judge those who are alive and also those who have died. God will wrap up the old, physical universe and create a new heaven and new earth that are exactly as he wants them to be – absolute perfection, the completion of his work in Jesus.

BIBLE BASE

Isaiah 65:17–25; 66:22; 2 Peter 3:10–13; Revelation 21:1–8,23–27

MATERIALS AND EQUIPMENT

For your own preparation and for other parts of the session, you'll need:

- your Leader Theme Card (page 7) and Bible
- an overhead projector and screen (optional)
- two slips of paper for each group member – an orange one and a yellow one
- five minutes' worth of clips from world TV news, with a mix of 'good news' and 'bad news' (use newspaper cuttings as an alternative source)
- TV and DVD
- pens
- your aristocrat's costume with binoculars (you just knew you'd need it again!)
- two Bibles
- thick felt-tip pens
- two sets of Revelation Character Cards (pages 69,70) enlarged onto A3 paper and cut up
- two 30 cm rulers
- a plastic or cardboard crown
- an enlarged version of the session **Symbol** and **Shout** (page 71) on overhead projector acetate or paper
- the Theme Scoreboard
- some gentle background music for the reading of Revelation 21:1–8,23–27
- gear for the best party you can arrange – music, balloons, streamers, food, drinks... whatever, but hide it until the **Scheme**.

PREPARATION

DO 'YOUR OWN TIME WITH GOD' (SEE BELOW). ALSO DO A BIT OF BACKGROUND READING ON REVELATION. FOR INSTANCE, TRY MICHAEL WILCOCK, THE MESSAGE OF REVELATION, IVP, 1984, OR GORDON D FEE AND DOUGLAS STUART, HOW TO READ THE BIBLE FOR ALL ITS WORTH, SCRIPTURE UNION, 1994 (CHAPTER 13), OR EUGENE H PETERSON, REVERSED THUNDER, HARPER COLLINS, 1991.

YOUR OWN TIME WITH GOD

God's story has no end, but this session examines the last chapter. First read Isaiah 65:17–25 and 66:22. The prophet Isaiah knew that, in the future, God's kingdom would come on earth. The whole of creation would be renewed, with a new heaven and new earth like the Garden of Eden – a new 'birth' that would encompass everything.

The New Testament makes it clear that Jesus will return to sort out those who trust in him and those who don't, and that God will create the new heaven and earth. Pause at the end of each verse of 2 Peter 3:10–13, to let it sink in. The detail of life in this new creation is breath-taking, as you will discover from Revelation 21:1–8,23–27. Christians have a secure place in it; the covenant is kept in the best possible way (verse 3).

READ
ISAIAH 65:17–25;
66:22; 2 PETER 3:10–13
REVELATION 21:1–8,
23–27

After exploring these Bible verses, thank God for what the future holds. Pray that your Christian group members will be encouraged to live confidently for God whatever happens, and that those who aren't yet Christians will want to say 'Yes' to Jesus as Lord of their lives.

| AD 75 | AD 100 | AD 125 | AD 150 |

BIBLE EVENTS

All dates approximate

AD 91–95   John probably writes Revelation some time during these years.

AD 130   The oldest known fragment of the New Testament – a scrap of John's Gospel – is copied.

OTHER WORLD EVENTS

AD 77   The Romans conquer Britain.

AD 79   The volcano Vesuvius erupts and destroys Pompeii.

AD 81   Domitian becomes emperor, calls himself 'master and god' and demands that people worship him.

AD 91–95   Domitian persecutes Christians fiercely.

AD 96   Domitian is assassinated; Nerva becomes emperor.

AD 122   Emperor Hadrian begins building a wall and defences in northern Britain.

AD 132   The independent state of Israel leads the Jews in revolt against the Romans; the Jews capture Jerusalem.

AD 135   The Romans crush the Jewish revolt; the Jews are driven out of Israel.

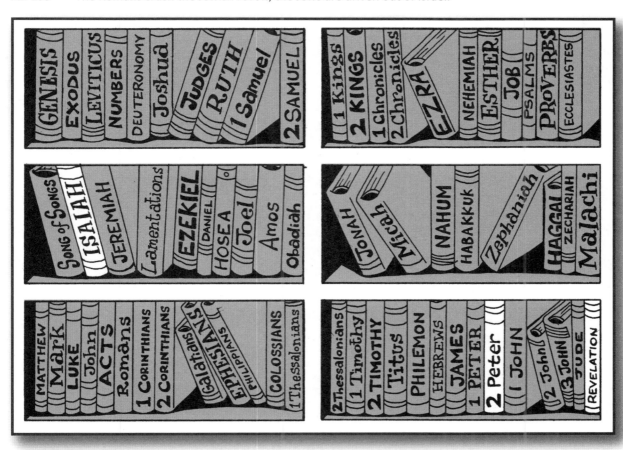

HANDY HINT

Young people in this age group may well be trying to work out if this 'faith in God' stuff is for them or not. Perhaps things will begin to fall into place during this session as they hear about Jesus coming back to take all the believers to be with him in the new heaven and earth. They may realise that they have been right to trust him all along and want to renew their commitment to him. Perhaps for the first time, they may want to place their lives into the safe hands of the One who has a vast plan that encompasses the past, present and future, and who wants the very best for them.

Be ready to spend time chatting with any who have questions or want to talk further about their own faith. Don't be pushy – they don't want or need to be pushed. Simply try to be aware and available, just in case.

Get a leader to dress as an aristocratic Isaiah with binoculars.

SCENE-SETTER

As group members arrive, hand them pens and orange and yellow slips of paper. Get them watching the video news items – or browsing through the newspaper cuttings. They should note on their orange slips (by writing or drawing) anything they see which isn't what God wants in the world, and on their yellow slips anything which is what God wants. Collect the slips and keep them in two piles for later.

Introduce the **Scheme** in this way:
Fast rewind to the Old Testament. Jerusalem is in ruins. God's people are in exile in Babylon, feeling totally insecure. Remember all that? It must have seemed as if the bad in the world had won, that the forces of evil had defeated God's people. Then the prophet Isaiah told them something to help them be bold and confident again.
Your aristocratic 'Isaiah' reads out Isaiah 65:17–25 and 66:22 in an authoritative manner.

Then continue: *New heavens and new earth? Well, not just yet. Fast forward to the last book of the Bible – Revelation. It was probably written by a man called John about sixty years after Jesus died. The Christians were being persecuted by the Romans. They'd begun to wonder who was stronger: God or the Romans? Then Jesus gave John an amazing vision full of unusual characters and breath-taking action. But who will win in the end? God or Satan? It's time to play 'Weird, wild and wonderful'.*

SCHEME

Instructions are on pages 69,70. After the game say:
One day Jesus will return to judge people according to whether they have said 'Yes' to him and belong to God, or have refused to have anything to do with him. And then what John saw will happen. Read out the words of Revelation 21:1–8,23–27 accompanied by some gentle background music.

So welcome to the Wild and Wonderful Party at the end of absolutely everything! This is where God's big plan has been heading all this time. In the new heaven and earth, everything weird, bad and wrong will have gone. God and his people will be together for ever. Bring on all the party goods. Hand back the 'Not what God wants' orange slips. All tear up the slips and, throw them into the air. Start the music. Eat, drink, and celebrate!

SYMBOL AND SHOUT

Show this session's **Symbol** as a backdrop to the party, and chant the **Shout** together (page 71). Even risk doing a conga to it so that everyone learns it by heart!

SCOREBOARD

Display the Theme Scoreboard. By now, everyone should know what to do and be ready to spot the themes. So don't stop the party but offer pens around with an invitation to write on the Scoreboard.

SPACE

During a quieter moment, get everyone to close their eyes. Say: *Imagine you're face to face with a bunch of tough Roman officials who tell you: 'Say "Caesar is lord!"… or else!' The penalty for not saying it could be death. But you know that Jesus is Lord, so what will you do? Spend two minutes thinking about it silently. Remember that God has won the victory already, even though there are still wrong things happening in the world. One day he will create a new heaven and earth for his people. So what do you want to say to him?*

Finish by going crazy with the 'Weird, wild and wonderful' **Shout** and conga.

At the heart of Revelation is a vision of our all-powerful God ruling over history. Good and evil clash on an epic scale. Below and on page 70 are some characters who play a key role, either on God's side or against him. Explain to your group members that they will meet some weird, wild and wonderful vision characters here.

1 Enlarge both these pages onto A3 paper or card and cut out the cards. Make two complete sets.

2 Mark the exact mid-point of your playing area and place the crown on it.

3 Divide your group into two teams. Stand them at opposite ends of the room but positioned one third of the way in from the wall. They should stand in a line, shoulder to shoulder, all facing the crown. (If you're pushed for space, play outdoors.) Ideally have one adult leader with each team.

4 Give each adult leader a Bible, a 30 cm ruler and one shuffled set of cards.

5 According to the size of your room, decide what a 'unit' (as used on the cards) will represent. It might be one ruler length, or two, or a half... whatever. Calculate it on the basis of your teams being twenty units from the crown. Describe a 'unit' to the team leaders.

6 On the word 'Go!' a team member picks a card and reads it out. Someone else in the team must read out all Bible verses quoted and find the missing character name. If the answer is correct, the team moves the number of units shown on the card in a straight line forwards or backwards. Then the next team member takes a card, and so on. It's a race!

7 The first team to reach the crown wins it and the game.

REVELATION CHARACTER CARDS

CHARACTER NAME

....

This character symbolises Jesus who gave his life as a sacrifice for all.

REVELATION 14:1

ON GOD'S SIDE, SO MOVE FORWARD SIX UNITS

CHARACTER NAME

....

These characters symbolise the coming of God's judgement.

REVELATION 8:1,2,6,7

ON GOD'S SIDE, SO MOVE FORWARD FOUR UNITS

CHARACTER NAME

....

This character symbolises God's people (the baby is the Messiah, God's chosen one).

REVELATION 12:1–2,5–6

ON GOD'S SIDE, SO MOVE FORWARD FIVE UNITS

REVELATION CHARACTER CARDS

CHARACTER NAME

This character has seven heads and ten horns, and represents Satan.

REVELATION 12:3,4,7–9

DEFINITELY NOT ON GOD'S SIDE, SO MOVE BACKWARD SIX UNITS

CHARACTER NAME

These characters symbolise anti-God powers.

REVELATION 3:1,11,12

DEFINITELY NOT ON GOD'S SIDE, SO MOVE BACKWARD THREE UNITS

CHARACTER NAME

These characters bring seven plagues like the exodus plagues.

REVELATION 15:1

ON GOD'S SIDE, SO MOVE FORWARD FOUR UNITS

CHARACTER NAME

This character symbolises the enemy of God's people, the city of Rome – or other power in the world that is against God.

REVELATION 17:1–2

DEFINITELY NOT ON GOD'S SIDE, SO MOVE BACKWARD TWO UNITS

CHARACTER NAME

This character represents the church, God's people. It's a woman.

REVELATION 19:6–8

ON GOD'S SIDE, SO MOVE FORWARD FIVE UNITS

CHARACTER NAME

This character represents the Son of God with fantastic power.

REVELATION 19:11–16

DEFINITELY ON GOD'S SIDE, SO MOVE FORWARD SIX UNITS

WEIRD, WILD AND WONDERFUL

NO MORE CRYING, NO MORE PAIN,
NO MORE DYING. SAY THAT AGAIN?
THERE'LL BE NO MORE SUFFERING,
NOTHING THAT'S WRONG
IN GOD'S NEW CREATION
WHERE YOU CAN BELONG.

THE WHOLE STORY

EVERYTHING IN ONE GO!

AIMS

To help group members:
- brush up the whole Bible story in outline
- locate themselves in God's vast plan for absolutely everything

SCOPE

The whole sweep of the Bible story

BIBLE BASE

Hebrews 1:1–4; 2:1–3; Revelation 21:3

MATERIALS AND EQUIPMENT

For 'Scribblaround':
- a roll of lining paper with the words of Hebrews 1:1–4 and 2:1–3 enlarged in the middle of it, with space left round the edge
- thick felt-tip pens

For 'Shout mega-mix':
- the acetates or enlarged versions of the **Shouts** from all the sessions
- an overhead projector and screen (optional)

For 'All together now!':
- parts of the Bible story (pages 74–76) enlarged to A3, cut up into individual strips and shuffled

For 'Absolutely Everything!':
- copies of the board game (pages 78,79) enlarged to A3 and stuck together down the middle, one copy for every three or four group members
- copies of the game rules (page 76)
- dice and counters

For 'The Bible in 50 words':
- copies of page 77, one for each group member

PREPARATION

HERE ARE FIVE WAYS OF RECAPPING ON THE WHOLE BIBLE STORY, AND OF ENCOURAGING YOUR GROUP MEMBERS TO THINK ABOUT WHAT IT MAY ALL MEAN FOR THEM. CHOOSE THE ACTIVITIES THAT WILL WORK BEST WITH YOUR GROUP — MAYBE ONLY ONE OR TWO OF THOSE GIVEN — OR PERHAPS RUN ALL THE ACTIVITIES AT THE SAME TIME, WITH EVERYONE DIVIDED INTO SMALL GROUPS. DO 'YOUR OWN TIME WITH GOD', THEN GET TOGETHER ALL THE MATERIALS YOU'LL NEED FOR THE SESSION.

YOUR OWN TIME WITH GOD

Christian educator Lawrence Richards has called the Bible 'God's invitation to us to experience reality'. In other words, what we see in its pages is the real world, real life and real values. What we actually experience day by day may be only a pale imitation of the reality we see there. But God has invited us to live and work with him in his amazing plan for absolutely everything. And he didn't just invite us by sending messages. Read Hebrews 1:1–4. You can tear up or delete a message, you can even shoot the messenger, but Jesus can't be ignored (verses 2,3).

Pray especially for any of your group members who as yet don't have a personal faith in Jesus. Even if they ignore the message or forget it, the truth of the message won't go away. Read Hebrews 2:1–3.

As you have worked your way through *Absolutely Everything!*, what has struck you in a fresh way about who God is and what he has done? Thank him for showing you this truth, and plan to share with your group something of what you have discovered.

READ
HEBREWS 1:1–4;
2:1–3;
REVELATION 21:3

 30

SCRIBBLAROUND

Lay out the sheet of lining paper on the floor, with the enlarged version of Hebrews 1:1–4 and 2:1–3 printed in the middle of it. Get everyone to sit round the edges of the paper. Ask a confident reader to read the verses aloud.

Discuss together what the verses tell you about:
• God the Father (like how he created everything, how he communicated with people)
• Jesus the Son (like who he is, his involvement in the past, present and future of everything)
• God 'creating', 'saving', 'showing who he is', 'promising' and 'judging'
• the choice about Jesus that everyone has

Get your group to remember Bible incidents that these verses remind them of. For instance:
• who were the 'prophets'?
• who were some of the 'ancestors'?
• what was God's 'message' for everyone?

Give everyone a pen. Invite them, all together in a scrum, to scribble in the border around the verses anything they have remembered from the *Absolutely Everything!* sessions. If possible, they should link it with a line to the Bible words that reminded them. They can draw instead of write, if they want.

Finally get everyone to walk slowly around the sheet reading everyone's comments and praising God silently for his amazing plan for absolutely everything. Invite them to talk to God about whether they are on his side in this plan or not, helping to get done what he wants in *his* way.

 30

SHOUT MEGA–MIX

Display all the **Shouts** one after the other in the right order, and challenge your group to learn the whole story by heart. It's tough but possible! Perhaps divide into teams to help each other learn it. Use only the title of each session to prompt them into chanting the appropriate **Shout**.

 30

ALL TOGETHER NOW!

Cut up all the pieces of the Bible story from A3 copies of pages 74–76. Shuffle and distribute them like playing cards around your group members. Challenge them as a whole team to lay out on the floor the complete Bible story, with all the pieces in the right order. Everyone must be responsible for putting down their own pieces rather than one person collecting them up and doing all the work.

If they have them all in the correct order, the letters on the sheets should read: 'God's home is now with his people. He will live with them...' (Revelation 21:3).

Explain how this moment in this verse is what the whole story of everything has been leading to – God living as close as possible to his people for ever. Also, indicate where the present moment in time is located, before Jesus' return, and help your group to look forward to all that is still to come.

 30

ABSOLUTELY EVERYTHING!

Divide your group into threes or fours. Give each small group a board game (pages 78,79), a dice, a set of rules (page 76), and enough counters for everyone. Let them play the game two or three times.

 30

THE BIBLE IN 50 WORDS

Give everyone a copy of the words on page 77. The group should learn it by heart and choose a way to perform it. As they do so, you could display the words on the overhead projector, if you wanted.

ALL TOGETHER NOW!

G — GOD CREATES THE UNIVERSE, WITH PEOPLE AS THE BEST OF CREATION.

O — PEOPLE CHOOSE TO DISOBEY GOD AND ARE SEPARATED FROM HIM.

D' — IN A FLOOD GOD WIPES OUT ALL LIVING THINGS, EXCEPT NOAH AND HIS FAMILY.

S — PEOPLE BECOME 'CIVILIZED' AND TRY TO LIVE WITHOUT GOD.

H — GOD TELLS ABRAM TO SET OUT FOR THE LAND THAT GOD WILL SHOW HIM. ABRAM OBEYS.

O — ABRAM ARRIVES IN CANAAN, THE PROMISED LAND.

M — GOD CHANGES ABRAM'S NAME TO ABRAHAM, MEANING 'FATHER OF MANY NATIONS' — THE BEGINNING OF THE FIRST COVENANT (AGREEMENT) WITH HIS PEOPLE.

E — ABRAHAM'S SON ISAAC LIVES IN CANAAN AS A SHEPHERD.

I — ABRAHAM'S GRANDSON JACOB LIVES IN CANAAN WITH HIS 12 SONS.

S — FAMINE HITS CANAAN. THERE'S NOT ENOUGH FOOD FOR JACOB'S LARGE FAMILY.

N — JACOB'S FAMILY MOVES TO EGYPT WHERE ONE OF THE SONS, JOSEPH, IS IN CHARGE OF THE CORN SUPPLIES.

O — JACOB'S DESCENDANTS LIVE IN EGYPT FOR 400 YEARS. THEY BECOME SLAVES TO THE EGYPTIANS.

W — GOD MAKES JACOB'S DESCENDANTS INTO A NATION, THE PEOPLE OF ISRAEL. 'ISRAEL' IS ANOTHER NAME FOR JACOB.

W — GOD SENDS MOSES TO GET HIS PEOPLE OUT OF EGYPT.

I — GOD GIVES THEM THE TEN COMMANDMENTS AND OTHER RULES FOR LIVING. NOW THEY REALLY ARE HIS PEOPLE.

T — ISRAEL ENTERS INTO A COVENANT WITH GOD. THEY ARE HIS PEOPLE, HE WILL PROTECT THEM, SO THEY PROMISE TO OBEY HIM.

H THE ISRAELITES CROSS THE RIVER JORDAN WITH JOSHUA AS THEIR LEADER, AND ENTER CANAAN, THEIR PROMISED LAND.

L DURING SOLOMON'S REIGN, ISRAEL ENJOYS PEACE AND PROSPERITY LIKE NEVER BEFORE.

H HOSTILE TRIBES IN CANAAN TRY TO GET RID OF THE ISRAELITES.

E SOLOMON'S SON REHOBOAM IS A HARSH KING. ONLY TWO TRIBES OF ISRAELITES (BENJAMIN AND JUDAH) WANT HIM AS KING. THE OTHER TEN ASK FOR JEROBOAM.

I THE ISRAELITES SETTLE IN CANAAN.

H ISRAEL SPLITS IN TWO. THE NORTHERN HALF OF THE COUNTRY IS NOW CALLED ISRAEL. THE SOUTHERN HALF IS CALLED JUDAH.

S GOD GIVES THE ISRAELITES JUDGES TO HELP THEM FIGHT AGAINST THE TRIBES THAT ARE ALREADY IN CANAAN. MOST JUDGES ARE SOLDIERS.

E THEN IN BOTH ISRAEL AND JUDAH THERE IS A SERIES OF RULERS. A FEW OF THEM OBEY GOD, BUT MOST OF THEM DON'T.

P THE LAST JUDGE IS SAMUEL, NOT A SOLDIER BUT A PROPHET, SOMEONE WHO TELLS GOD'S PEOPLE WHAT HE WANTS THEM TO KNOW.

W THE ASSYRIANS ATTACK ISRAEL AND TAKE THE PEOPLE CAPTIVE.

E THE PEOPLE SAY THEY WANT A KING. SAMUEL REMINDS THEM THAT GOD IS THEIR KING, SO THEY DON'T NEED ANY OTHER.

I THE BABYLONIANS ATTACK JUDAH, DESTROY JERUSALEM AND TAKE THE SURVIVORS TO BABYLONIA.

O GOD LETS THE ISRAELITES HAVE A KING, SAUL.

L THE PERSIANS RELEASE GOD'S PEOPLE FROM BABYLONIA. MANY, INCLUDING NEHEMIAH, RETURN TO JERUSALEM TO REBUILD THE WALLS AND TEMPLE. THEY WAIT FOR GOD'S CHOSEN KING.

P AFTER SAUL, ISRAEL HAS TWO BRILLIANT KINGS – DAVID THEN HIS SON SOLOMON.

L AROUND FOUR HUNDRED YEARS LATER, JESUS IS BORN TO SAVE PEOPLE FROM THE WRONG THAT SEPARATES THEM FROM GOD.

L JESUS TEACHES AND HEALS, TELLING AND SHOWING PEOPLE THE GOOD NEWS OF GOD'S KINGDOM.

I JESUS DIES SO THAT ALL WHO BELIEVE IN HIM CAN BECOME GOD'S PEOPLE.

V GOD RAISES JESUS FROM DEATH. THE GOOD NEWS OF JESUS IS FOR EVERYONE.

E JESUS RETURNS TO HEAVEN.

W GOD SENDS THE HOLY SPIRIT TO HELP JESUS' FOLLOWERS. THE CHURCH IS BORN.

I SAUL, A PHARISEE, ARRESTS JESUS' FOLLOWERS AND THROWS THEM IN PRISON.

T SAUL HIMSELF BECOMES A FOLLOWER OF JESUS AND IS CALLED PAUL INSTEAD.

H PAUL TRAVELS THREE TIMES ROUND THE MEDITERRANEAN LANDS WITH THE GOOD NEWS OF JESUS.

T MORE AND MORE PEOPLE TRUST JESUS. BUT THE ROMANS MAKE LIFE HARD FOR CHRISTIANS, AND KILL SOME OF THEM.

H TODAY THE NUMBER OF GOD'S PEOPLE IS STILL GROWING.

E ONE DAY JESUS WILL RETURN.

M GOD WILL MAKE A NEW HEAVEN AND A NEW EARTH. ALL HIS PEOPLE WILL BE WITH HIM FOREVER, AS CLOSE TO HIM AS POSSIBLE.

RULES FOR PLAYING 'ABSOLUTELY EVERYTHING!'

- You will need a game board, a dice, and a counter for each player.
- The aim of the game is to reach heaven and to be with God for ever.
- Each player throws the dice. The player with the highest score goes first, then passes the dice to the person on his or her left. You don't need to throw a six to start. Play continues in a clockwise direction.

- As you move your counter, read out loud all the squares you jump over, as well as the one you land on. If you forget, you miss your next turn.
- You need to throw the exact number to finish.
- Keep playing until everyone has reached the new heaven and new earth.
- If you have time when everyone has finished, play again.

THE BIBLE IN 50 WORDS

GOD MADE
ADAM BIT
NOAH ARKED
ABRAHAM SPLIT
JACOB FOOLED
JOSEPH RULED
BUSH TALKED
MOSES BALKED
PHARAOH PLAGUED
PEOPLE WALKED
SEA DIVIDED
TABLETS GUIDED
PROMISE LANDED
SAUL FREAKED
DAVID PEEKED
PROPHETS WARNED
JESUS BORN
GOD WALKED
LOVE TALKED
ANGER CRUCIFIED
HOPE DIED
LOVE ROSE
SPIRIT FLAMED
WORD SPREAD
GOD REMAINED

(Source unknown)

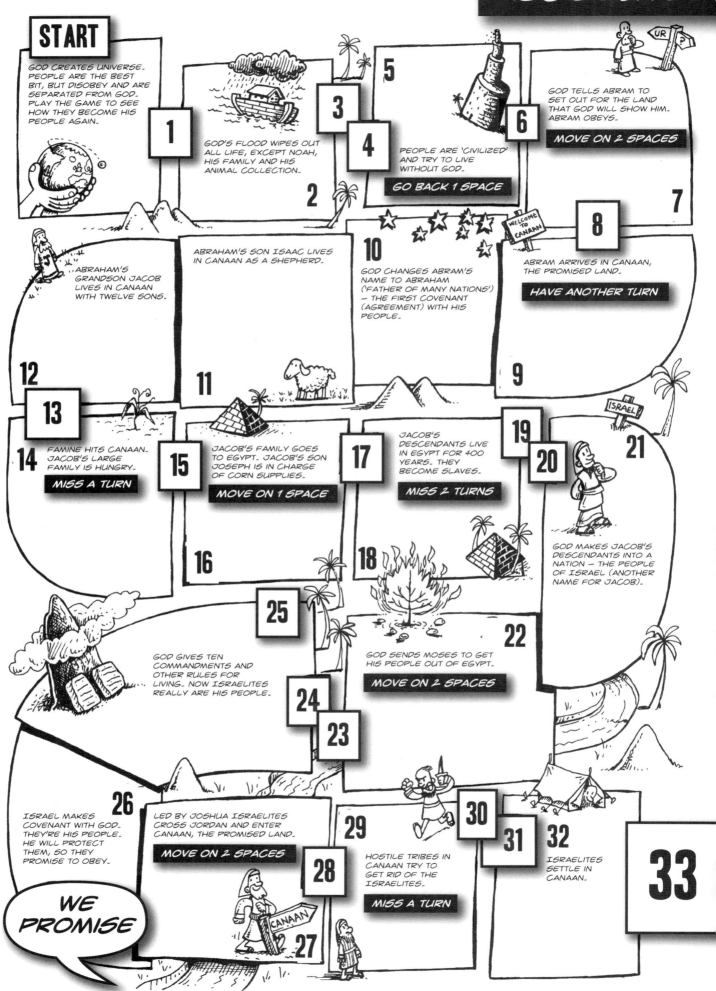

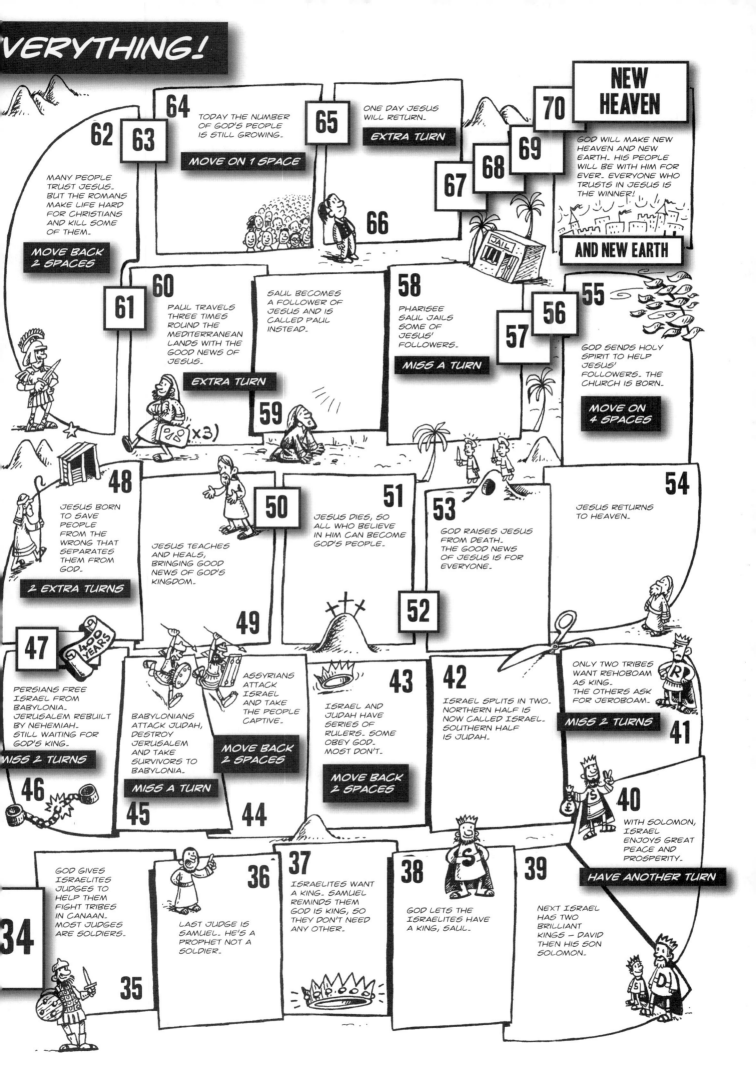

70 NEW HEAVEN

GOD WILL MAKE NEW HEAVEN AND NEW EARTH. HIS PEOPLE WILL BE WITH HIM FOR EVER. EVERYONE WHO TRUSTS IN JESUS IS THE WINNER!

AND NEW EARTH

69

68

67

64

TODAY THE NUMBER OF GOD'S PEOPLE IS STILL GROWING.

MOVE ON 1 SPACE

65

ONE DAY JESUS WILL RETURN.

EXTRA TURN

66

62 **63**

MANY PEOPLE TRUST JESUS. BUT THE ROMANS MAKE LIFE HARD FOR CHRISTIANS AND KILL SOME OF THEM.

MOVE BACK 2 SPACES

61

60

PAUL TRAVELS THREE TIMES ROUND THE MEDITERRANEAN LANDS WITH THE GOOD NEWS OF JESUS.

EXTRA TURN

(x3)

59

SAUL BECOMES A FOLLOWER OF JESUS AND IS CALLED PAUL INSTEAD.

58

PHARISEE SAUL JAILS SOME OF JESUS' FOLLOWERS.

MISS A TURN

57 **56**

55

GOD SENDS HOLY SPIRIT TO HELP JESUS' FOLLOWERS. THE CHURCH IS BORN.

MOVE ON 4 SPACES

JAIL

48

JESUS BORN TO SAVE PEOPLE FROM THE WRONG THAT SEPARATES THEM FROM GOD.

2 EXTRA TURNS

50

JESUS TEACHES AND HEALS, BRINGING GOOD NEWS OF GOD'S KINGDOM.

51

JESUS DIES, SO ALL WHO BELIEVE IN HIM CAN BECOME GOD'S PEOPLE.

53

GOD RAISES JESUS FROM DEATH. THE GOOD NEWS OF JESUS IS FOR EVERYONE.

54

JESUS RETURNS TO HEAVEN.

49

52

47 400 YEARS

PERSIANS FREE ISRAEL FROM BABYLONIA. JERUSALEM REBUILT BY NEHEMIAH. STILL WAITING FOR GOD'S KING.

MISS 2 TURNS

46

45

BABYLONIANS ATTACK JUDAH, DESTROY JERUSALEM AND TAKE SURVIVORS TO BABYLONIA.

MISS A TURN

44

ASSYRIANS ATTACK ISRAEL AND TAKE THE PEOPLE CAPTIVE.

MOVE BACK 2 SPACES

43

ISRAEL AND JUDAH HAVE SERIES OF RULERS. SOME OBEY GOD. MOST DON'T.

MOVE BACK 2 SPACES

42

ISRAEL SPLITS IN TWO. NORTHERN HALF IS NOW CALLED ISRAEL. SOUTHERN HALF IS JUDAH.

ONLY TWO TRIBES WANT REHOBOAM AS KING. THE OTHERS ASK FOR JEROBOAM.

MISS 2 TURNS

41

40

WITH SOLOMON, ISRAEL ENJOYS GREAT PEACE AND PROSPERITY.

HAVE ANOTHER TURN

34

GOD GIVES ISRAELITES JUDGES TO HELP THEM FIGHT TRIBES IN CANAAN. MOST JUDGES ARE SOLDIERS.

35

36

LAST JUDGE IS SAMUEL. HE'S A PROPHET NOT A SOLDIER.

37

ISRAELITES WANT A KING. SAMUEL REMINDS THEM GOD IS KING, SO THEY DON'T NEED ANY OTHER.

38

GOD LETS THE ISRAELITES HAVE A KING, SAUL.

39

NEXT ISRAEL HAS TWO BRILLIANT KINGS – DAVID THEN HIS SON SOLOMON.

RESOURCES

theGrid
For 11–14s – every quarter

Discipleship resource for church groups, adaptable for different backgrounds: from those who are on fire for God to those who don't want to be there. *theGrid* is also on www.lightlive.org

TOP TIPS

Easy-to-read guides to aspects of youth work
Written by people who have lots of experience in theology and youth work, these books give the biblical background, and then explore what it means in practice. Each book ends with ten top tips!

- EXPLORING THE BIBLE WITH YOUNG PEOPLE
- EXPLAINING THE TRINITY TO YOUNG PEOPLE
- LEADING SMALL GROUPS

WORKING WITH 11 TO 14s
Pretty much everything you need to know

Does what it says on the tin! This book is full of useful theory and practical advice on working with this rewarding age group. Celebrate the joys and work through some of the difficulties as you explore ministry with 11 to 14s.

YOU&GOD
Elaine Carr

This interactive book brings different prayer ideas to life for young people aged 11 to 14. The book is designed to help them pray for different areas of their lives in a variety of different ways.

FRIENDS FIRST
Claire Pedrick and Andy Morgan

Packed full of advice for young people about relationships of all kinds – from romance to your gran!

THE CHOCOLATE TEAPOT
David Lawrence

Guides 11 to 14s through the pressures of school, so they won't melt like a chocolate teapot when the going gets tough!

WHAT NOW?

What Now? has been produced with the fine people at Soul Survivor. It's an essential guide to some of the core stuff of Christianity and is ideal for young people who have just made a decision to follow Christ. With advice, teaching and real-life stories, this is a great grounding in what it means to be a Christian.

THE LOST BOOK TRILOGY
Kathy Lee

Jamie and Rob live far in the future, when the seas have taken over and turned mountains into islands. Their life is simple until they find a book in a sealskin bag. What is the book? And what is the message it contains? Three exciting adventure books.

- THE BOOK OF SECRETS
- THE BOOK OF GOOD AND EVIL
- THE BOOK OF LIFE

THE 'NO' SERIES
Kathy Lee

Charlie, Emma, Rachel and Abena are angels at church, but in school, well, that's a different matter. These three books explore three of their stories, of how these girls are challenged to live as Christians throughout their lives, not just on a Sunday.

- NO ANGEL
- NO MEANS NO
- NO LOVE LOST

DARK CHAPTERS

In the Dark Chapters series, some of the darker stories from the Bible are retold to help young people discover more about God. These books provide a credible Christian alternative to the multitude of horror titles available to young people.

- THE EGYPTIAN NIGHTMARE – the story of Pharaoh and the plagues, by Hannah MacFarlane
- THE SKY WILL FALL – the story of Samson, by Darren R Hill
- IZEVEL, QUEEN OF DARKNESS – the story of Jezebel, by Kate Chamberlayne
- THE ONCOMING STORM – the story of Noah, by Andrew R Guyatt
- BABYLON – the story of Daniel, by Hannah MacFarlane